IRONMAN'S

ULTIMATE GUIDE TO NATURAL

BODYBUILDING

IRONMAN'S

ULTIMATE GUIDE TO NATURAL
BODYBUILDING

IRONMAN MAGAZINE AND PETER SISCO

CB

CONTEMPORARY BOOKS

Library of Congress Cataloging-in-Publication Data

Ironman's ultimate guide to natural bodybuilding / Ironman magazine
    and Peter Sisco [editor].
        p.   cm. — (Ironman series; bk.4)
    Includes index.
    ISBN 0-8092-2814-9
    1. Bodybuilding. I. Sisco, Peter. II. Series.
GV546.I76   2000
646.7′5—dc21   00-20120
                                        CIP

Cover design by Todd Petersen
Cover photograph copyright © Michael Neveux. All rights reserved.
Cover models: Mike O'Hearn and Christina Bybee
Interior design by Hespenheide Design

Published by Contemporary Books
A division of NTC/Contemporary Publishing Group, Inc.
4255 West Touhy Avenue, Lincolnwood (Chicago), Illinois 60712-1975 U.S.A.
Copyright © 2000 by *Ironman* magazine and Power Factor Publishing, Inc.
Printed in the United States of America
International Standard Book Number: 0-8092-2814-9

00 01 02 03 04 05 VL 19 18 17 16 15 14 13 12 11 10 9 8 7 6 5 4 3 2 1

CONTENTS

FOREWORD

Ironman magazine was founded in 1936 by Peary and Mabel Rader of Alliance, Nebraska. Their first print run of 50 copies was done via a duplicating machine that sat on their dining room table. *Ironman* started out as an educational vehicle to inform and enlighten those people who were interested in weight lifting, bodybuilding, and, eventually, powerlifting.

The focus of *Ironman* magazine during its first 50 years was on all three sports, with emphasis on weight training in general as a life-enhancing activity. *Ironman* has always stressed the health and character-building aspects of weight training and has always been the leader in bringing exercise and nutrition concepts and ideas to those in the training world.

In the early '50s, *Ironman* magazine was the first weight-training publication to show women working out with weights as part of their overall fitness regimen. It even went so far as to show a pregnant woman training with weights and educating readers on the benefits of exercise during pregnancy—thoroughly modern concepts 25 years ahead of its time. In the late '50s and early '60s, *Ironman* magazine was the first to talk about high-quality proteins derived from milk and eggs as well as liquid amino acids. The bimonthly magazine had, by this time, acquired over 30,000 subscribers simply on the strength of its information. The Raders never worked at expanding its circulation. It grew by word of mouth fueled by the general hunger for and *Ironman*'s ability to provide intelligent, timely, and reliable training information.

By the early '80s, the Raders, now in their 70s, had spent nearly 50 years working incredibly long hours to put out a bimonthly publication. The hard work was beginning to take its toll.

I'd been interested in *Ironman* as a business since the mid-'70s and had in fact talked several times with the Raders about purchasing *Ironman*. Eventually, my dream of owning and publishing a bodybuilding magazine was realized, and in August 1986, after 50 years, *Ironman* magazine changed owners. At that time, *Ironman* had a circulation of 30,000 subscribers, had no foreign editions, was published bimonthly, and averaged 96 black-and-white pages, with a color cover. Fourteen years later, *Ironman* magazine is published worldwide with an English-language circulation of 225,000 and additional editions in Japanese, Italian, German, Arabic, and Russian.

The books in the *Ironman* series represent the "best of the best" articles from over 60 years of *Ironman* magazine.

John Balik
Publisher, Ironman

ACKNOWLEDGMENTS

I would like to thank the following people who made this book possible:

John Balik, publisher of *Ironman* magazine, had the foresight to see the need for this book and the others in the *Ironman* series. His knowledge of bodybuilding and his sensitivity to the information required by readers has made *Ironman* the best bodybuilding magazine in the world.

Steve Holman, editor in chief of *Ironman*, creates one informative, insightful issue of the magazine after another, and his own articles in this book show ample evidence of his innovation and encyclopedic knowledge of the iron game.

Mike Neveux is the premier bodybuilding photographer in the world. His photos in this book and in every issue of *Ironman* magazine have inspired and motivated countless bodybuilders around the world by capturing the intensity, power, and magnificence of these great athletes.

A special thanks to Terry Bratcher, art director of *Ironman*, who did an enormous amount of work in the preparation of this book by wading through *Ironman*'s immense archive of articles and photographs in order to help bring you the "best of the best."

A special thanks, also, to Christina Bybee and Mike O'Hearn for generously posing for the front-cover photo of this book. Mike is a champion natural bodybuilder, powerlifter, and martial artist. He is the star of the "Battle Dome" television series and is active in the charity organization Bodybuilders Against Hunger.

Finally, I would like to thank all the writers who contributed to this book. These writers have an incalculable collective knowledge of the sport of bodybuilding. This book represents the distilled knowledge of hundreds of man-years of study in every aspect and nuance of the iron game. Between the covers of this book are wisdom and experience that would cost a small fortune to obtain from one-on-one training with these writers. Sadly, some are no longer with us to be able to share their vast insights, making their advice in these pages all the more valuable. It is the thought, effort, and writing of these individuals that make this book and *Ironman* magazine great.

Peter Sisco
Editor

INTRODUCTION

Congratulations on your choice to be a natural bodybuilder. It's a wise one. *Ironman's Ultimate Guide to Natural Bodybuilding* is designed to help you make the best gains possible without chemicals so you reap all the benefits sensible bodybuilding has to offer, including better health and more self-confidence as your physique develops.

This book will guide you with techniques, routines, and information you can use to be successful at building your physique without chemicals. One way to learn the ropes is to look to bodybuilders who have excelled in drug-free competitions, like the men and women who win the NPC Team Universe competition each year. Some of them are featured on the following pages. Keep in mind, however, that most of these athletes have been training for years and have exceptional genet-

ics as well, so you may have to make adjustments to some of their wisdom to fit your specific genetic inheritance.

There's really no getting around the fact that you have to experiment in the gym to continue making gains in size and strength. That's why we present a diverse range of information from many bodybuilding experts, along with the strategies of drug-free competitors. You essentially must become your own lab rat, trying different split routines, experimenting with new exercises and machines, and testing the intensity waters. Do that and be consistent with your training, and you'll be rewarded with great gains, a muscular physique, and a lifetime of successful workouts.

John Balik
Publisher, Ironman

IRONMAN'S

ULTIMATE GUIDE TO NATURAL

BODYBUILDING

Brad Hall and Amy Lynn.

Chapter 1

THE BODYBUILDING LIFESTYLE
A HEALTHY GOLD MINE

BY DANIEL CURTIS

Not everyone who bodybuilds competes. In fact, the majority of bodybuilders train to look and feel better, which they do. The benefits don't stop there, however.

Take a look at the effect bodybuilding can have on heart disease, the number-one killer in the United States. The contributing causes include smoking, genetic factors, high blood pressure, obesity, sedentary lifestyle, and elevated serum lipid levels (cholesterol and triglycerides). While bodybuilding can't stop you from smoking or change your genetics, the bodybuilding lifestyle, including diet, can help with the other items listed above.

Regular workouts translate into weight loss, decreased blood pressure levels, and positive changes in lipid profiles, all of which adds up to a possible decrease in the incidence of heart disease. According to an article that appeared in a 1984 issue of the *Journal of the American Medical Association*, "Few investigators have considered the consequence of exercise using resistance to muscular movement (weight lifting), despite evidence suggesting that periodic, intense muscular activity of the heavy-work occupations may reduce the incidence of coronary (heart) disease."

The researchers undertook a study to see how 16 weeks of weight training affected lipid and lipoprotein levels in previously sedentary men, average age 33, and women, average age 27. The subjects trained three days per week, every other day, for 45 to 60 minutes per workout. The routine included bench presses, seated rows, lat pulldowns, military presses, leg presses, leg extensions, leg curls, and arm curls. The subjects performed 3 sets of each exercise for as many reps as possible, taking a maximum of two minutes' rest between sets. Once they could get out 8 reps, the weight was increased by 10 to 15 pounds.

The results were impressive. In the men the harmful low-density-lipoprotein, or LDL, cholesterol was reduced by 16.2 percent, while it was reduced by 17.9 percent in the women. The beneficial high-density-lipoprotein, or HDL, cholesterol increased—something that's very difficult to accomplish in men. In fact, it

Jim Shiebler.

average of 55 milligrams per deciliter, comparable to that of joggers. The powerlifters also had a higher level of the harmful LDL cholesterol, a 138-milligrams-per-deciliter average compared to a 104 average for the bodybuilders. The article concluded that "the training regimen of bodybuilders is associated with a more favorable lipid profile than the training used by powerlifters." In other words, the kind of weightlifting bodybuilders do is far more beneficial to the heart than the kind powerlifters do.

When the subjects used steroids, the HDL cholesterol decreased in both groups by an average of 55 percent and the LDL level increased by 61 percent, resulting in the obvious conclusion that "steroid use by strength-trained athletes may increase risk for coronary heart disease."

Even in the face of an atherogenic diet—that is, one that's likely to promote heart

went up a whopping 15.8 percent in the male subjects and only 4.8 in the females. The authors concluded that "weight-training exercise appears to result in favorable changes in lipid and lipoprotein levels in previously sedentary men and women." This is big news for a public that's been told for years that only endurance exercise can benefit the heart. The researchers felt that the incredible increase in HDL cholesterol in men "may have been due to the reduction in bodyfat, along with the increases in lean body mass (muscle)."

How does bodybuilding-type weight training stack up against powerlifting-type training when it comes to improving health? A 1984 study compared the two to see which form was healthier. The study, which also appeared in the *Journal of the American Medical Association*, looked at steroids and their effect on health as well. Prior to using steroids, the powerlifters in the study had an average HDL cholesterol of 38 milligrams per deciliter while those who had practiced bodybuilding, again without using steroids, had a very favorable

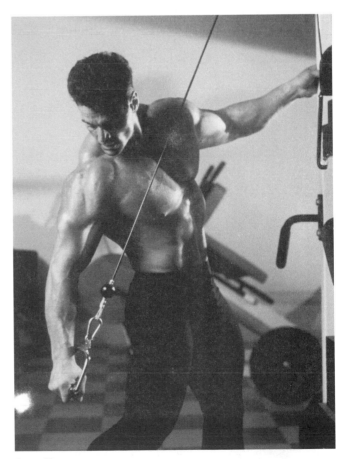

Greg Blount.

disease—the bodybuilders come up healthy. A 1986 study that was published in the *International Journal of Sports Medicine* looked at bodybuilders who consumed more than six eggs per day and concluded that their lipid profiles were very favorable. HDL cholesterol was higher than average, and triglycerides and the harmful LDL cholesterol were not elevated.

What about all the protein that bodybuilders typically consume? Many physicians and nutritional experts complain that bodybuilders take in excessive amounts of protein, labeling it unnecessary and harmful to the kidneys. In my 20 years of working in at least a half dozen different hospitals, I've never seen a bodybuilder admitted with kidney disease or

kidney failure. Nor, for that matter, have I ever seen one with heart disease or read in the medical literature about bodybuilders suffering from ill health due to a high-protein diet. In fact, in all those years I've only seen two bodybuilders in the hospital. One had suffered a pec tear when the bench broke under him, and the other was admitted due to amphetamine abuse. It may be dangerous—and it's certainly unnecessary—for someone who isn't a bodybuilder to ingest large amounts of protein, especially without also taking in adequate fluids, but for practicing bodybuilders it doesn't seem to be a problem.

Provided you don't use steroids or other drugs, bodybuilding offers a number of excellent health benefits—and not just physical ones. In a study titled "Muscular Strength: A Predictor of Personality in Males," which was published in a 1983 issue of the *International Journal of Sports Medicine*, researchers set out to determine the psychological implications of bodybuilding. They quoted numerous studies involving aerobic exercise and concluded that the results were conflicting. Some showed a positive effect psychologically, while others did not. What was missing was information regarding strength training and its effect on a person's psychological state.

The researchers tested 142 college students before and after an exercise period that consisted of squats and bench presses. The results suggested that "relative muscular strength is a significant predictor of personality" and that "relatively strong young men tend to be significantly more satisfied with their body-parts and processes; less emotionally labile and anxious; more outgoing, sociable, and impulsive; and more confident and satisfied with themselves in general than were their muscularly weaker counterparts."

Young men and women should be strongly encouraged to consider bodybuilding as part of their lives. There is more to be built than just muscles. Confidence, self-worth, and self-esteem are also important benefits, and they translate into greater success in school, work, and social relationships.

Indeed, bodybuilding offers a veritable gold mine of total health.

Steve Cuevas.

Chapter 2

BEGINNING BODYBUILDING
THREE DAYS A WEEK

BY MIKE TORCHIA

This is a three-days-per-week bodybuilding routine. In this type of program you train three times a week—for example, on Monday, Wednesday, and Friday—dividing up the bodyparts so that you train your entire body once during the week. I have chosen the following variation on a traditional bodypart split:

Day 1 (Monday): Abs, chest, and triceps
Day 2 (Wednesday): Abs, legs, calves, and shoulders
Day 3 (Friday): Abs, back, and biceps

Abdominal exercises provide a great warm-up and strengthen your lower back, bracing it for your workout. You may want to start with a general warm-up of six minutes maximum on the treadmill or stationary bike before you move on to the ab work. Save your cardio session for after the weight training, however, because any more than a few minutes drains your muscles of glycogen, the carbohydrate-based fuel you need to power your workout.

Themis Klarides.

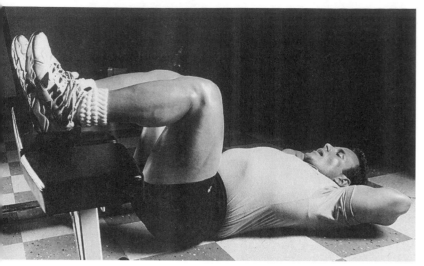

Crunch—start position.

Crunch—finish position.

poundage and dropping the number of reps on each successive set. Whenever the workout calls for sets of "15, 12, 10," pyramid the weight and drop the reps accordingly. In any event, note that the program also calls for 3 sets on all exercises.

At the end of each weight-training workout do 30 minutes of cardiovascular exercise. I believe the treadmill is the top piece of equipment for this. Take long, lunging steps, landing on your heels, to work your glutes hard. Cardio is an important element in a fitness program because it burns unwanted bodyfat, which enables you to see the results of your weight training more clearly.

Finally, finish off your workout with a good stretch. This aids recuperation, which is essential to muscle growth.

To train your entire body completely and effectively and keep your training stimulating, alternate the following two programs on a weekly basis.

Squat—start position.   Mike Torchia.

The program is designed for variety, with two workouts for each training day and a selection of exercises involving dumbbells, barbells, and machines. This enables you to condition your body with different types of resistance exercise. The free weights will not only stimulate increased muscle mass and power, but they'll increase your coordination and balance as well, a benefit you don't get from most machines.

The workouts also introduce the technique of pyramiding, in which you increase the intensity of exercise by upping the

Squat—finish position.

PROGRAM A

Workout 1: Abs, chest, and triceps

Crunches	3 × 20
Lying bent-knee leg raises	3 × 20
Incline dumbbell presses	3 × 15, 12, 10
Flat-bench dumbbell flyes	3 × 15, 12, 10
Cable pushdowns	3 × 15, 12, 10
Lying triceps extensions	3 × 15, 12, 10
Treadmill	× 30 minutes
Stretch	

Workout 2: Abs, legs, calves, and shoulders

Crunches	3 × 20
Hanging leg raises	3 × max
Leg extensions	3 × 15, 12, 10
Squats	3 × 15, 12, 10
Standing calf raises*	4 × 25
Seated dumbbell presses	3 × 15, 12, 10
Dumbbell lateral raises	3 × 15, 12, 10
Recumbent bicycle	× 30 minutes

*Two sets with toes pointing in and two with toes pointing out.

Triceps extension—start position.

Triceps extension—finish position.

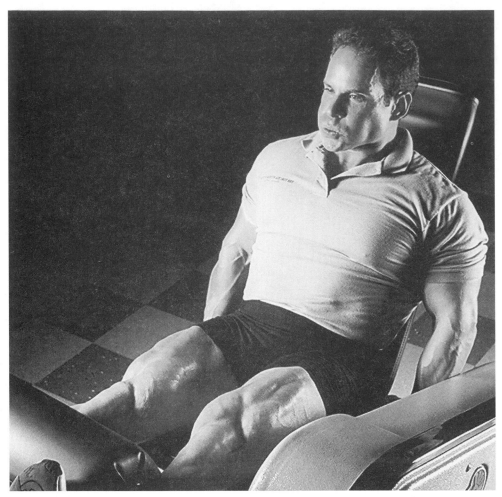

Leg extensions.

Incline situp—start position.

Incline situp—finish position.

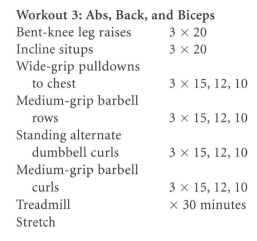

Workout 3: Abs, Back, and Biceps

Bent-knee leg raises	3 × 20
Incline situps	3 × 20
Wide-grip pulldowns to chest	3 × 15, 12, 10
Medium-grip barbell rows	3 × 15, 12, 10
Standing alternate dumbbell curls	3 × 15, 12, 10
Medium-grip barbell curls	3 × 15, 12, 10
Treadmill	× 30 minutes
Stretch	

Pulldowns—start position.

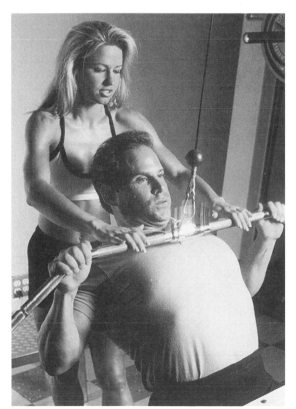

Pulldowns—finish position.

Stretch.

PROGRAM B

Workout 1: Abs, Chest, and Triceps

Crunches	3 × 20
Lying bent-knee leg raises	3 × 20
Flat-bench dumbbell presses	3 × 15, 12, 10
Incline dumbbell flyes	3 × 15, 12, 10
Close-grip bench presses	3 × 15, 12, 10
Dumbbell kickbacks	3 × 15, 12, 10
Recumbent bicycle	× 30 minutes
Stretch	

Workout 2: Abs, Legs, Calves, and Shoulders

Crunches	3 × 20
Hanging leg raises	3 × max
Leg curls	3 × 15, 12, 10
Leg presses	3 × 15, 12, 10
Seated calf raises*	4 × 25
Barbell front presses	3 × 15, 12, 10
Barbell upright rows	3 × 15, 12, 10
Treadmill	× 30 minutes
Stretch	

*Two sets with toes pointing in and two with toes pointing out.

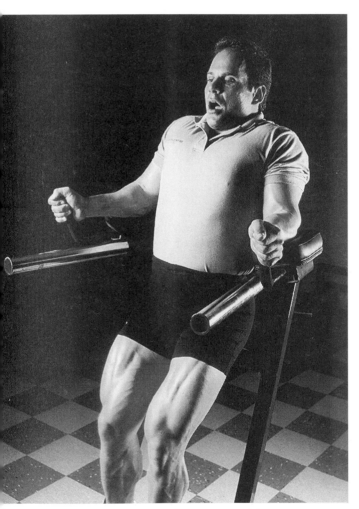

Hanging leg raises—start position.

Hanging leg raises—finish position.

Workout 3: Abs, back, and biceps

Bent-knee leg raises	3 × 20
Incline situps	3 × 20
Close-grip chins or pulldowns to chest	3 × 15, 12, 10
One-arm dumbbell rows	3 × 15, 12, 10
Close-grip preacher curls	3 × 15, 12, 10
One-arm dumbbell concentration curls	3 × 15, 12, 10
Recumbent bicycle	× 30 minutes
Stretch	

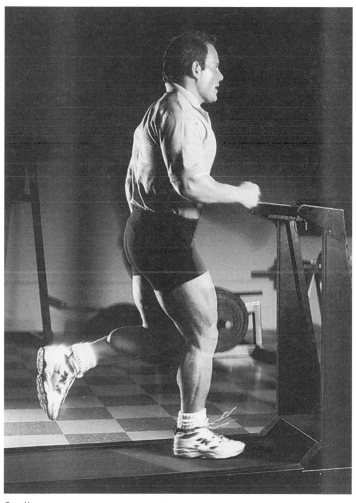

Cardio.

Skip La Cour.

Chapter 3

LEAN, CLEAN MASS MACHINE
HOW DRUG-FREE BODYBUILDER SKIP LA COUR GROWS PHYSICALLY, EMOTIONALLY, AND SPIRITUALLY

BY STEVE HOLMAN

At 5′10″, 232 pounds of solid, drug-free muscle—in contest shape, mind you—Skip La Cour has more pressing concerns than just buying clothes that fit. He's constantly fending off accusations that he's a 'roid head. It used to bother him, but now he takes it in stride. And why shouldn't he? He's doing what he loves and making a good living, and he truly believes he's only scratched the surface of his genetic potential. When you have that kind of confidence, not even finger pointing by the envious, no matter how loudly they scream, can shake your drive and determination. Skip is focused on becoming the best drug-free bodybuilder in the world, and he's doing it with hard work, scientific supplementation, and a will of iron.

Let's delve a little deeper into the mind-set of this genetic marvel so that you can take on of some of his "mass machine" attitude and squeeze more success from your own bodybuilding endeavors.

IM: OK, Skip, let's clear the air right off the bat. Are you really drug-free?

SLC: Absolutely, but I understand where people are coming from when they have doubts. If I'd seen someone in the magazines who looked like me when I had only a couple of years of training experience, I would've thought the same thing.

Natural bodybuilding is too new to be fully understood right now. Although I'm very proud of what I've accomplished with my physique, I realize I can get much better. I also realize I'm not the best natural bodybuilder in the world; however, I've marketed myself very well and have created opportunities. I stick out from the pack because I'm a heavyweight and because of the publicity I round up for myself.

I also understand that my achievements as a natural bodybuilder threaten other bodybuilders' certainty and significance. In the past they were certain that they were on the right path, they were certain that only so much could be achieved without drugs, and they were certain that they had to take drugs to become really successful in the sport. They used to think they were very good drug-free bodybuilders. Because of that they could feel

One-arm row.

Leg extensions.

as if they were doing the right thing when they took drugs to fulfill their dreams and feel significant. I challenge all of those beliefs—and many people don't want to accept that.

IM: As a drug-free bodybuilder you must have a lot of contempt for the drug-using pros, correct?

SLC: No, I try not to pass judgment on those people. I understand that if I was 19, earning only slightly more than minimum wage, using recreational drugs every so often—and if I wasn't so darn cheap—steroids might be an option. But that's not me. I believe that bodybuilding is about promoting a healthy lifestyle and that part of living a healthy life is having a healthy attitude. Having compassion, understanding, and empathy for others is part of being a good human being. Natural bodybuilders should be firm in their commitment but ease up on passing judgment on others.

Barbell curls.

I also believe that natural bodybuilders should take full responsibility for their own progress. We shouldn't blame the guys on drugs for our inferior development, and we shouldn't blame poor genetics. We should do whatever we can to find the combination of strategies that will make us become the best we can be. We need to keep the pressure on ourselves because that challenge is what's going to make us realize our full genetic potential.

IM: Speaking of genetic potential, let's backtrack a bit so people realize that yours is in the "super" category. How did you get involved in bodybuilding, how much weight did you put on in the beginning, and how long did it take you to win your first contest?

SLC: I started bodybuilding when I was 27, nine years ago. I had relocated for my job, and I didn't know anybody, so my upstairs neighbor suggested I join a gym. Once I started training regularly, I grew like crazy. I was a pretty lean 190 before I started, and I gained 30 pounds of muscle in six months.

When that happened, I heard all the stories and rumors about me being on drugs. I remember one guy saying to me, "You're taking those Flintstone vitamins, aren't you?" I had no clue what he was talking about.

I entered my first show at a ripped 200 pounds and won the Overall just 13 months after I started training. Being new to bodybuilding, I didn't know it was such a big deal until a lot of people around town started approaching me.

The next weekend I entered and won a drug-tested show. I found out later that the contest officials spent all of the contestants' drug-testing money to run my urine through every possible test for drugs.

Then a fairly influential person in the sport at that time told me there was the possibility that I could become a professional bodybuilder within a couple of years. I was initially thrilled—until I started asking a few questions, like, "How much money do pro bodybuilders make?" The man just laughed. I was making a pretty decent living at the time and had no intention of going backward financially.

Then I asked, "Will I have to take drugs?" He laughed again. I wasn't dead set against drugs until he told me they'd cost around $500 a month.

At that time steroids weren't controlled substances, and you could get around the law by having a doctor prescribe them for you. But the man's source had been arrested for improperly prescribing steroids. I'd never been in trouble with the law, and there was no way I was going to start at age 30.

From that point on I put my head down and focused on becoming the best natural bodybuilder in the world.

IM: What do you say to the critics who claim you could do almost anything and still grow naturally because of your genetics?

SLC: Although I've been very blessed, genetics don't get your butt out of bed at 3:30 in the morning to prepare your food and clothes for the day, to go to the gym and train with some very heavy weight, to go to work for a stressful 10 hours, to go back to the gym for cardio work at night and immediately return home afterward to do the same routine over again, day after day, week after week, month after month. Genetics don't make you willingly accept the sacrifice of short-term gratification in order to achieve long-term fulfillment. Genetics don't give you the determination to continue to go for your dreams when others—and sometimes even your own mind—try to tell you they're impossible to achieve. Genetics don't keep you plugging along when it seems as if there's a world of negative people who criticize you and try to drag you down to the life of mediocrity they're unfortunately settling for.

There are many examples of bodybuilders with above-average genetics who have done nothing in this sport because they haven't had the drive, passion, or perseverance.

Isn't it interesting that the critics will say my development is the product of either great genetics or illegal drugs—never considering the possibility of hard work or advanced knowledge in training, nutrition, and supplementation?

Barbell rows.

IM: I know you take a lot of supplements, so what's your opinion of the new pro-hormones like androstenedione? Do you consider them drugs?

SLC: My philosophy has always been that if a supplement is legal, I can use it and remain drug-free. I don't believe that if you use the pro-hormones you are doing anything unethical—at least, unless they become banned by the bodybuilding organizations or made illegal.

I just recently started taking androstenedione. I waited because some of the people I look to for information told me it might be harmful—but that's apparently false.

IM: What's your attitude about protein intake for bodybuilders, and how many grams do you take in a day?

Pullups.

SLC: Protein is the number-one nutrient you need to build your muscles. Muscle is protein. Without protein you're going to have a very hard time growing muscle.

You always want to maintain a positive nitrogen balance. That means you absolutely must consume more nitrogen than you excrete—keeping your body in a positive protein-accrual environment.

I find the more protein I consume, the bigger and stronger I get. I ingest approximately 453 grams of protein a day. About 165 grams (36 percent) come from regular food while 288 (64 percent) come from high-quality whey protein in meal replacements and powder. I spread this over eight meals.

I understand that cost plays a major role in many bodybuilders' food and supplement budgets. Because of that I'd say that 1 to 1 1/2 grams per pound of bodyweight is what the average hard-training bodybuilder needs per day.

IM: You talked earlier about bodybuilders taking responsibility for their own gains—or lack of gains. What about hardgainers?

SLC: Some people go so far as to attach the identity of hardgainer to being natural, so they become "hardgaining natural bodybuilders." How empowering an identity is that?

When someone tells me they're a hardgainer, I ask, "Compared to whom?" There's always someone who's going to come along who'll make you look like a hardgainer. There are bodybuilders who make me look like a hardgainer. At the same time, I'm sure you can build muscle faster than some people out there. You have to look at how so-called hardgainers approach training. Do they attack it with confidence and certainty? Do they feel that the next strategy or method will launch them into a new level of growth? Are they excited to get to the gym because they know the hard work is going to pay off in a big way?

Hardgainers usually believe that regardless of methods or amount of effort, they can only achieve minimal results. Referring to yourself with a disempowering label such as "hardgainer" is definitely something you should reconsider.

Why would people want to assume such a disempowering identity? They put themselves in a can't-lose situation. If they achieve measurable gains, they win. If they don't, they blame the fact that they're hardgainers. In other words, it's not their fault.

That's also the reason most drug-free bodybuilders are so adamant about announcing their drug-free status. It's like saying, "The reason I'm not as big as other guys is because I'm natural."

I received a letter from a guy in Florida named Dave Grillo. Dave earned a black belt in martial arts and has been training with weights for 10 years. He has a great attitude and didn't even tell me in our first few conversations that he has cerebral palsy—oh, and no legs. I hope people like Dave can inspire us all to get the most out of ourselves. Think about him the next time you call yourself a hardgainer. He has the opportunity to call himself one, but he chooses not to.

IM: How many sets should drug-free bodybuilders be doing per bodypart?

SLC: Probably a lot less than the majority of us are currently doing. As I get wiser and more experienced, I find myself doing less and less; however, you can't quantify the number of sets per bodypart without emphasizing the word *intensity*.

Intensity to me means extremely heavy weight used in a goal-oriented, determined, and focused manner. Now, I realize the majority of bodybuilders feel they're training heavy and with a lot of intensity. I want to remind them—and everyone—that there's always a higher level to aspire to! I don't care what you accomplished in the past or how much weight you lifted, you can always accomplish and lift more. Adopting that belief will keep you training with optimal intensity.

If people are really pushing themselves hard and using heavy enough weights to truly overload the muscles, 6 sets is enough for most bodyparts. That, of course, is after they warm up sufficiently. For some bodyparts 4 is enough. For the back, because there are so many different muscles, 8 is a good number of sets.

You must strive to become the best you can be and appreciate what you've accomplished.

IM: Is training each bodypart once per week the way to go for the majority of drug-free bodybuilders?

SLC: I highly recommend it. I implemented that system at the recommendation of Paul Delia, of AST Research, in 1994, right after the NPC Team Universe. Just 13 weeks later, 6 pounds heavier and considerably harder, I won the Musclemania Natural Bodybuilding Championships. One year later, 17 pounds heavier and in better condition, I won the Heavyweight class at the Team Universe. What makes it more amazing is that this development occurred after I'd already been training for six years. People often get those kinds of gains when they first begin training, but not after so many years. The only other factor besides switching from a three-on/one-off routine was that I started taking creatine at the same time.

I don't spend a lot of time learning about all the great things that steroids do, but I do know one of their biggest benefits is that they help you recover a lot sooner. The sooner you recover, the sooner you can train that muscle again. The more you can efficiently train the muscle, the bigger it will get.

I think it would be safe to say that most natural bodybuilders overtrain—including myself from time to time. If you don't wait to train a muscle group until it's fully recovered, you'll minimize your efficiency. The one-bodypart-once-a-week training schedule allows natural bodybuilders to recover from their workouts sufficiently. They're also well rested from the previous week to train with maximum intensity—both from a physical and mental standpoint. [See "Skip La Cour's One-Hit-Per-Bodypart-Per-Week Split" on page 23 for details.]

IM: So what's your advice for up-and-coming drug-free bodybuilders who see the drug users getting bigger by the week?

SLC: To concentrate on becoming the best they can be. Many get frustrated when they see a person who's significantly better than they are. I know this from personal experience. Recently, I had the opportunity to spend some time observing peak-performance specialist Anthony Robbins. He's young, energetic, handsome, intelligent, passionate, and very wealthy. He's a total giver, loves people, and helps them make gigantic changes in the quality of their lives.

For the next three days I was borderline depressed. I felt that compared to Robbins my life has been a total waste of time, that my accomplishments were nothing compared to his. I thought I was losing this game of life, although I'm doing very well at it.

I realize now that there's always a higher level of accomplishment to reach—and there will always be someone better at whatever you're good at, someone bigger, stronger, wealthier, or better looking. You must focus on yourself. You must strive to become the best you can be and appreciate what you've accomplished to truly experience happiness.

IM: It sounds as if you've figured out a lot of things and really have your head on straight. What are your goals now?

SLC: My ultimate goals in bodybuilding are broken down into two categories: competitor and professional businessperson.

As a competitor I want to win the Team Universe and represent the United States in international competition. I want to represent the United States at the Olympic Games when bodybuilding becomes an official sport.

As a businessperson I'd like to provide information and inspiration to bodybuilders around the world who are trying to build the best physique they can. I plan on accomplishing this through my articles, books, website, and seminars.

In a nutshell, my goals are to become an outstanding bodybuilder and a great physique- and mind-development coach.

Arnold Schwarzenegger said during a television interview that he's successful because he's "hungry and fearless." That's a mind-set I've modeled from the Oak to help me accomplish my goals.

SKIP LA COUR'S ONE-HIT-PER-BODYPART-PER-WEEK SPLIT

Day 1: Shoulders
Day 2: Back
Day 3: Quadriceps
Day 4: Chest
Day 5: Arms
Day 6: Hamstrings
Day 7: Rest

He trains his calves and abdominals three to four times per week.

Sample Delt Routine:

Barbell presses	6 × 12, 10, 8, 6, 4–6, 4–6
Dumbbell presses	2 × 4–6
Dumbbell laterals	3 × 12, 4–6, 4–6
Bent-over laterals	2 × 4–6

James "Broadway" Bivens.

Chapter 4

THE (NOT-SO) MEAN, CLEAN MUSCLE MACHINE

BY LONNIE TEPER

I got my first look at James Bivens one January night in 1989. I was teaching a bodybuilding course at California State University, Los Angeles, and, while the students were pacing through their routines, I was on the alert for possible candidates for the school's bodybuilding championships, which I produced annually from '84 to '94. Since the contestants had to be current CSULA students, let's just say I wasn't too picky. Anyone better than me would do, actually. If that.

Midway through the class an imposing 6′2¹/₂″, 245-pound male strolled through the facility. He was checking out the equipment. I immediately began checking for my contest application forms. He said he wanted to add the course. I said I wanted to add him to the contest lineup. The soft-spoken 20-year-old apologized. He'd love to compete, he said, but he was on a track scholarship and was the school's number-one shot-putter and discus thrower. Bivens didn't think the coaches would approve of his preparing for my show at the same time. He was right.

I learned that Bivens had transferred to Cal State from Long Beach City College. He'd gone to high school in West Palm Beach, Florida—the same school Burt Reynolds attended—where he'd been a starting lineman on the football team and the state champion in the discus.

I knew I had to get this prodigy in my contest, if not that season, then in the future. James Bivens was a bodybuilding champion waiting to happen. His extraordinary genetic gifts included a waist smaller than my mother's, Lee Haney–type pecs, and a front lat spread that would have put many in the sport to bed. I asked him why in the world he would want to go out to the track on hot, smoggy days and throw a 16-pound steel ball around when he could be on stage in posing trunks, winning titles, and getting dates with women.

"Listen," I told the guy, "you can be a good college shot-putter or a great bodybuilder. I think that if you work hard at this game, your name will be in lights someday." Thus, the instantaneous moniker Broadway Bivens.

At age 17, 6′2″, 200 lbs.

Age 20, 6′2½″, 310 lbs.

James liked what he heard, agreed that tossing a ball was boring and that he'd finish out the current track season, then concentrate on shaping his physique. His coaches hated me, especially after Bivens placed second in the shot-put event in the highly competitive California Collegiate Athletic Association with a best of 54′6″. Surely he'd have been a threat for a national title the following year. I could see, though, that lifting iron, not throwing it, was his true calling.

As he'd promised, Bivens dropped out of track after the season and set his sights on the bodybuilding contest that would be held on campus on February 10, 1990. With Elvis singing and Shawn Ray and Tonya Knight guest posing, it wasn't hard to fire Broadway up.

Bivens, weighing 220 pounds, placed third, behind Donald Potts, the Armed Forces Heavyweight titlist at the time, and Ed Kim, a 5′11″, 153-pound medical student.

He was staggered by his defeat at first, especially the loss to Kim, who, James thought, looked more like a skeleton than a second-place winner in a bodybuilding contest.

He announced his retirement the next week but, after inhaling three pizzas, calmed down and was ready to learn from his mistakes. "I didn't know what I was doing at that point," Bivens admitted recently. "My diet was crazy—I was just eating three bowls of Cream of Wheat and some Chinese food each day. My training was crazy, and I didn't understand the importance of sharpness and proportion over just size. In the long run losing that show, especially losing to someone as small as Ed, gave me a lot of insight about the sport. I lost 25 pounds for the contest, and most of it was muscle. Ed *should* have beaten me—he was much, much sharper and was more professional on stage. I did everything wrong, and I got what I deserved."

Bivens began attending as many local contests as possible and came to the conclusion that he'd never get anywhere against today's competition without the assistance of anabolic steroids. "I took my first cycle in July

1991," he said, "and cycled on and off for about four years. I never took growth hormone. I took my last drug in May of 1995, preparing for the Florida State Championships [he placed third at 263 pounds] and am proud to say that I've stayed drug-free—it's been over three years now."

The second-oldest of four children produced by James and Leona Bivens, James was born in Houston, spent the next five years in Bridgeport, Connecticut, and was raised primarily in Tampa, Florida. The summer prior to his junior year in high school his family moved to West Palm Beach. James Sr., a former pro football player and now a minister, supplied the genetics that James Jr. has gratefully made the most of. "At his biggest my dad was about 6′2″ and 250 pounds—and that's without lifting weights," he said.

Bivens was a standout 218-pound football player who got lost in the shuffle playing on a team that only won a single game his senior year. "We were so bad," he said with a laugh, "we only won four games in the two years I played."

He was originally pushed into pumping iron by his father. "He knew I was going to play football in high school and that lifting weights would benefit me tremendously," Bivens said. "I started lifting at home after my dad made me a bench out of a piece of wood. I was only 13 years old, and I really hated it in the beginning. But my father kept on pushing, and then I started to see some results. I was about 5′10″ and 140 pounds at the time. I graduated from high school in 1986 at 220 pounds."

James landed at Long Beach City College the following year when the school's noted track coach, Ron Allice, now the head man at the University of Southern California, wanted Bivens and Chris Wilcox, a great decathlete, to venture west. "I always had dreams about going to California, and this was my opportunity," Bivens said.

He moved back to his parents' home in the summer of '94 and in '96 trekked south to Miami Beach, where he's currently a personal trainer and does security work for local night clubs. At about the same time he decided to move away from the steroid route.

"I was strongly encouraged by someone I respect in the industry who told me that, with my genetics and strength I could go a lot farther in the sport as a drug-free athlete," Bivens said. "He kept reminding me of the health-related problems associated with drug usage, as well as the legal aspect. We have a history of high blood pressure in my family as

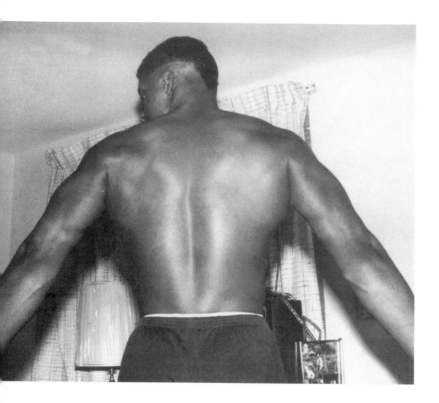

it is, so at that point I was ready to try things totally clean."

Bivens is proof that you can maintain size and strength going it the natural way. He finished third at the AAU Mr. America in October '97, although several claimed the show was definitely a battle between James and eventual winner Bill Davey.

After coming in at a sharp but still too stringy 254 pounds and finishing seventh at the '97 Team Universe, Bivens concluded that he needed to be at least 265 by the next time he appeared on stage. He kept training and kept growing—growing, in fact, to an unheard-of 315 pounds after the first of the year, displaying a condition that's not exactly chopped liver. "I decided to take a month away from the gym," he said. "I'd always believed that you had to train six, seven days a week. I would do as many as 25 sets for large bodyparts and 15 to 20 sets for smaller bodyparts.

"I began to realize that I couldn't train the way I did when I was on steroids; it obviously takes much longer to recover. So I started working out differently—extremely heavy,

with more rest days. I kept my rep range from 5 to 8 and I only did 8 to 10 sets for large bodyparts and 6 to 8 sets for small bodyparts.

"I started training three to four times a week, basically hitting each bodypart once every seven or eight days. Another key factor was that I started eating five to six meals a day in the off-season, not just precontest. I consume 7,000 to 8,000 calories a day, which I didn't come close to in the past, and I also supplement my diet with creatine, whey protein, and beta-hydroxy-metylbutyrate (HMB).

"Also, I'm eating more quality foods in the off-season—steak, chicken, lots of pasta. Even though I'm taking in a lot of calories, I'm keeping a closer eye on the types of foods I eat. Before, I would eat anything in sight just to total a certain number of calories so I could put on the weight. But it wasn't quality and I would put on too much bodyfat."

As a result, Bivens has packed on 55 pounds, much of it muscle, in the past $3^{1}/_{2}$ months, and his lifts are still about on a par with the poundages he pushed when he was on the sauce (the most Bivens weighed on drugs was 310). In certain cases he's even stronger now. Some of his more impressive

James Bivens and Lonnie Teper.

current numbers include the following: bench press—505 for a double, 315 for 22 reps; incline dumbbell press—160 for 8–10; squat—600 (below parallel); leg press—1,100 for 10–12 (deep reps); hack squat—650 for 10 (deep reps); lying triceps extensions—225 for 8.

More mind-boggling statistics: Bivens's recent measurements include a 57-inch chest, 22-inch arms, 32-inch thighs, and 18-inch forearms. In contest shape his waist gets down to 32 inches. He asked me not to publish his calf size—18$^1/2$ inches—oops. Hey, nobody's perfect, James. "I stopped doing calves at the

gym last year," he confessed. "They've been the same size now for a while. I've been doing 1,000 reps at home with my bodyweight a couple of times a week lately, although I'm sure I'll be getting back to heavy weights for my calves too. I'm just trying something different.

"I feel that eventually, perhaps in another year or two, I can look as good as I did at the Florida, weighing somewhere in the mid-260s, and still be sharp."

During his precontest phase Bivens turns it up just a notch, hitting each bodypart every four or five days but still keeping his total sets to 12 at most. "I try to lift heavy year-round," he said. "As far as supplements go, I'd recommend creatine as the best for the natural bodybuilder. It keeps the muscle full and keeps your strength up. I take creatine with HMB and a good protein powder, like a high-calorie weight gainer. I would say 3,000 of my calories come from shakes.

"I also do some cardio year-round now, as compared to only precontest in the past, and about 16 weeks out I'll start using the Stairmaster and treadmill on almost a daily basis for about 45 minutes.

"For the time being, 315 is about as big as I can get without getting sloppy, so I'm going to try and maintain before cutting back in preparation for my next show. I plan on doing something in the late fall, either the Mr. America again or the Musclemania. Hopefully, I will be 265 on stage and in my best condition. Remember, I just turned 30, and for those who think that's old, look again. Robert Washington [the '97 Team Universe Overall champion] was his best ever last year at 35, 36 years old. Rodney Davis [third at the Team Universe and Heavyweight winner at the '97 Musclemania] is about the same age. All of the top Light Heavies, like Milton Holloway and Darrell Monson, are in their mid-30s. Skip La Cour is another guy around 35 or 36, so I'm just beginning and don't expect to reach my full potential for a while yet.

"The drug-free bodybuilder has to learn to be patient. Things aren't going to come as easy or as fast. You can't let that get you down. I keep telling myself that Rome wasn't built in a day, and neither is a championship drug-free physique. I have to admit I get frustrated at times, especially when I have people telling me I can be 350 on drugs and around 300 in contest condition.

"But, as my adviser pointed out, there are a lot of 300-pound guys walking around on drugs. What does it mean? I want to achieve what no one has ever done before—prove that a drug-free bodybuilder can be as big and hard as someone on steroids and that you don't need drugs to push really heavy weight. It just

takes time and patience. If I can do it, so can other people."

Bivens feels he can show a good amount of muscularity at around 290 if promoters are interested in hiring him for guest-posing stints. "Let's put it this way," he says, "I will look a lot better at 290, drug-free, than a lot of today's pros do when they guest pose."

He says he'll also return to the Team Universe as soon as the National Physique Committee (NPC) adds the Super Heavyweight

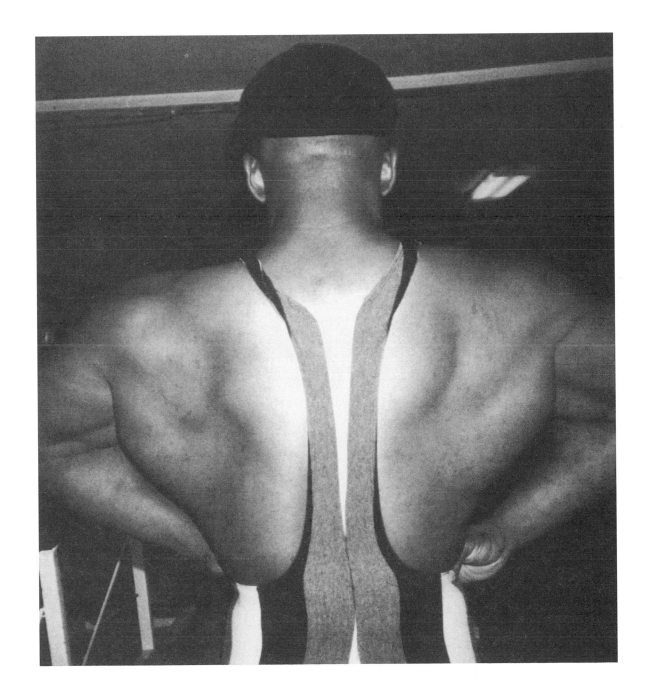

His last time on drugs: 263 pounds at the '95 Florida Championships.

division. The way this guy keeps packing on muscle, a Super-Dooper Heavyweight class might be more appropriate.

Oh, and how about my promise concerning all the ladies flocking around Broadway once he became a physique artist? Well, isn't a den full of trophies enough for now?

MEAN, CLEAN MUSCLE MACHINE TRAINING

Monday: Legs

Leg presses	4 × 8–13
Hack squats	4 × 6 × 8
Leg extensions	4 × 10–12
Seated leg curls	4 × 10–12
Lying leg curls	4 × 10–12

Tuesday: Chest and Biceps

Incline dumbbell presses	4 × 6–10
Hammer Strength presses	4 × 8–10
Dumbbell flyes	4 × 8 × 10
Alternate dumbbell curls	3 × 6–8
Machine preacher curls	3 × 8–10

Wednesday: Off

Thursday: Shoulders and Traps

Bent-over lateral raises	4 × 10–12
Seated dumbbell presses	4 × 6–8
Dumbbell shrugs	4 × 10–12
Pushdowns	5 × 6–10
Lying EZ-curl bar extensions	5 × 6–10

Friday: Off

Saturday: Back and Calves

Pullups (bodyweight)	3 × 10
Barbell rows	3 × 6–8
T-bar rows	3 × 8–10
Lat pulldowns	3 × 10
Donkey calf raises*	4 × 10
Seated calf raises*	4 × 15

*When he trains at the gym.

Every Other Day: Abs

Crunches	1 × 200

Cardio work

Bivens favors the Stairmaster and treadmill for cardio training. He does 30 minutes four to five times per week in the off-season, then, 16 weeks before a show, he ups it to 30 to 45 minutes six days a week.

OFF-SEASON MASS-BUILDING DIET

Meal 1
    2–3 cups oatmeal
    6 egg whites
    2 scoops whey protein powder
    1 banana
    5 grams creatine

Meal 2
    8 ounces (220 grams) pasta
    8 ounces ground sirloin
    2 cups mixed vegetables

Meal 3 (after workout)
    12-ounce chicken breast
    8 ounces pasta
    5 grams creatine

Meal 4
    1 protein shake*

Meal 5
    1 protein shake

*He consumes about two-thirds of a serving, 1,600–1,700 calories.

Will Willis.

Chapter 5

GET SMART
SHORT BUT SWEET ARM TRAINING WITH WILL WILLIS

BY RUTH SILVERMAN

"I've finally gotten smart," declared World Natural Bodybuilding Federation (WNBF) pro Will Willis. The drug-free bodybuilder was talking about his decision to open a private training gym, but he might well have been talking about his arm training over the years. When it comes to loading the guns he displayed in winning the '93 ABCC Natural California and taking second at the '94 WNBF Mr. Universe, he said, "I know that Will Willis's arm workouts in the beginning were a lot longer than they are now.

"I was like a lot of people—you have a strong bodypart, you want to train it all the time," continued Willis, who also admitted, "I was flexing my biceps way back in elementary school." His genetic predisposition for big arms got a considerable push during his teenage career in gymnastics, during which he won the Montana state championship on the parallel bars in his sophomore year. "Everything you do in gymnastics pretty much involves triceps," he observed. "My biceps grew

from all the iron crosses, and triceps from all the parallel bar and pommel horse work."

Consequently, when he started weight training during the summer before his senior year in high school, it wasn't long before he was doing 15 to 20 sets each—as many as four or five exercises—for biceps and triceps. He trained that way until he was 21, when after-the-show conversations with bodybuilding judges wised him up to the fact that he was starting to look like Popeye.

"Symmetry is my thing now," explained Willis, who was the National Physique Committee (NPC) Regional Teen Bodybuilder of the Year in Northern California in 1983 and who responded to the constructive criticism by limiting his arm training for a full year. He'd been working arms twice a week. He cut back to once a week, if that, doing maybe 3 light pumping sets for each bodypart for maintenance. He focused on bringing his chest and back into balance and figured his biceps and triceps were getting plenty of indirect work.

Eventually he switched to competing in the Amateur Athletic Union (AAU) and returned to blasting his arms. He was preparing for national-level competition and "wanted to be as extremely built as possible." The result was a string of victories culminating with a win at the '87 Mr. USA.

Willis dropped out of bodybuilding competition—and stopped weight training seriously for a couple of years in the late '80s, a period of personal growth during which he became very involved in his church. He started training clients—and training for competition again—in 1991, earning pro status in the WNBF, which requires athletes to be drug-free for at least seven years.

Although his main focus these days is getting his company, Ironwill Private Training, off the ground, the 5'11", 193-pound Willis is in shape year-round for modeling jobs and never far from contest condition. "You get me on a little bit of phosphagen and a few weeks of hard training and I'm ready to compete," he said. "I'm a little tighter than what I was before.

Concentration curls.

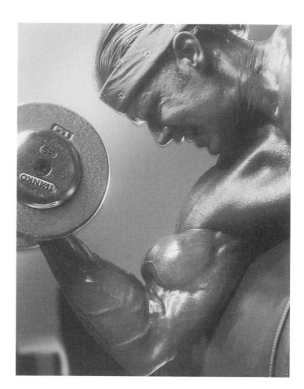

I've got a 29-inch waist. My chest still measures 49, so I've got a 20-inch difference . . . [and my biceps are] taping at 18½, which is pretty good for a natural guy."

Veteran bodybuilding photographer Russ Warner once compared Willis's rear double-biceps to that of Arnold Schwarzenegger "because I have the five different heads that lead up to that peak at the top."

Nowadays Will hits his biceps and triceps on separate days once a week as part of a four-days-on/three-off schedule. Here's his bodypart split:

Day 1: Chest and Biceps
Day 2: Legs and Calves
Day 3: Back
Day 4: Shoulders and Triceps

With his busy schedule of training clients, Willis does his own weight workout in the evening. He does abs and cardio on Days 1 and 3 in the morning and engages in some form of heavy cardiovascular activity, like in-line skating or mountain biking, on two of his off days.

In his bodypart routines Willis likes to rotate exercises; for example, he breaks up a couple of sets of alternate dumbbell curls with a set of concentration curls. He also likes to do what he calls pyramiding down in weight. After the first heavy exercise, on which he goes up in weight and down in reps, he often does the opposite—starts with his heaviest weight and works up in reps.

WILL BUILDS BICEPS

Lately, Willis has been organizing his biceps workout around preacher curls. "Those seem to peak my biceps," he said. "They hit the outer head really well. They hit the inner head at the top of the movement. I get a good stretch on the outer head at the bottom. I keep my elbows in real tight, and I get a real good peak when I hit a full contraction."

As part of his maintenance program Willis alternates heavy and light weeks on biceps training, but he goes heavy on the barbell preacher curls even on his light week.

A typical Will Willis biceps workout starts with a few light sets of standing barbell curls. "I don't do those heavy anymore, because my back can't take it," he said, "but they make a great warm-up." He does 6 to 7 work sets for

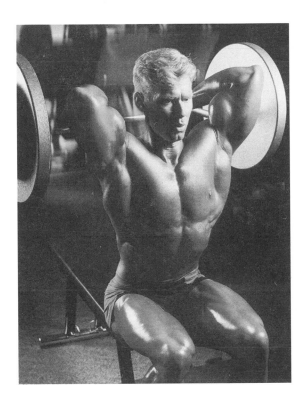

biceps on Day 1 after performing 12 to 15 sets for chest.

Here's a typical program for his heavy week. (For his light week he does 20 to 25

reps on 2 sets of concentration curls and rotates them with 1 set of down-the-racks on the alternate dumbbell curls.)

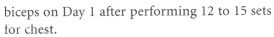

Barbell curls.

Dumbbell preacher curls.

WILL'S BICEPS BLAST

Warm-up
Standing barbell curls   2 × 15–20
Dumbbell curls   1 × 15–20

Work sets
Barbell preacher curls   3–4 × 4–8

Rotate exercises:*
Alternate dumbbell curls 2 × 10
Concentration curls   1 × 20

*One set of dumbbell curls, followed by concentration curls, followed by the other set of dumbbell curls.

WILL TRAINS TRICEPS

For this muscle group Willis favors seated one-arm dumbbell extensions, as well as seated barbell extensions, on which he brings the bar back behind his neck. "I get the best stretch on my triceps with those particular exercises," he observed.

"I really don't do a lot of close grip, because the outer part of my triceps is really well developed. I think that sometimes if you're too developed in that area, it takes away from the look of the arm."

For triceps work he also sticks with 6 to 7 work sets, which follow 12 to 15 sets for shoulders.

Here's a typical heavy-week workout.

WILL'S TRICEPS TOASTER

Rotate exercises:*
Seated one-arm dumbbell
    extensions   3 × 20, 15, 10
Pressdowns or lying triceps
    extensions   2 × 10–12
Seated barbell
    extensions**   2 × 8–10

*One set of one-arm dumbbell extensions, followed by a set of pressdowns, followed by a set of one-arm dumbbell extensions, etc.

**Behind the neck.

A ROUTINE FOR ALL SEASONS

Willis generally starts his clients out on higher reps and fewer sets for arm training. Aside from beginners, however, he believes the above routines "would be good for anyone who wants to build as well as maintain and for anyone who's on drugs or off drugs." The lesson he learned about arm training seems to be the trend. The results of his less-is-more approach are hard to miss.

"I've been looking at other natural bodybuilders. I think our bodies are a little more worn," he added. "We've already gotten ourselves to the optimum level, where we don't need to be in the gym for two or three hours a day to reach the kind of goals we did when we were younger." One thing Will Willis has learned throughout his training days is that he gets the same effect after an hour and 15 minutes of training as he got two years ago—as relative to even eight years ago—after three hours of training.

Lying triceps extensions.

Symmetry is Will Willis's thing now.

Steve Cuevas and Patricia Tomlinsen.

Chapter 6

GOOD WILL PUMPING

BY LONNIE TEPER

As a 15-year-old on his Temple City, California, Babe Ruth baseball team, Steve Cuevas was so puny he could have passed for the bat boy—or, perhaps, the bat. At 5'10" and 126 pounds, Cuevas might have replaced Kevin Costner as the title characters in *Thin Cup* and *The Post*.

I mean, this cat was to skinny what Notorious B.I.G. was to obese. He was so slight, in fact, that when the catcher took the last spot on the end of the bench, he didn't even realize he'd knocked little Stevie into the dirt with a slight bump on the rump.

Being tossed to the ground with the greatest of ease wasn't the final straw, however. It was watching, day in and day out, assistant coach Shannon Kirkpatrick drive to practice in his handsome sports car with a lovely lass by his side. Kirkpatrick, a 6'2", 225-pound former all-American football player at Steve's alma mater, Temple City High School, was often seen wearing a pair of tight shorts that showed off his physique, and Cuevas was so inspired

he began pumping iron at home and at the high school weight room. He also started following the famous see-food diet—on which he ate everything he saw.

"I was so obsessed with getting bigger and more muscular that I really didn't know what I was doing for the first year and a half or so," said Cuevas, who now sports a solid 220 pounds on his 5'11" frame, which he cuts back to 195 for contests. "I really overtrained. The first year I think I worked chest 364 out of 365 days. I worked out every single day, much of the time training twice a day. I wasn't exposed to a lot of the bodybuilding magazines back then, and when I did read something like *Muscle & Fitness*, they had all these routines the pros did. Basically, I was pretty much spinning my wheels."

When Cuevas graduated from high school, he was still tipping the scales at a paltry 157 pounds. By that time, though, he'd begun to read the magazines, and he'd learned that the first thing he needed to do was to put the

barbells down, not lift them. He'd had enough of being a dumbbell when it came to proper workouts.

"I took three months off, which was really hard to do," Cuevas said. "Boy, just thinking about taking a few days off was frightening. But I knew I had to do something drastic. So when I graduated [in 1984], I took the entire summer off." Upon his return to the gym, Cuevas was not only aided by a better knowledge of bodybuilding, but he was also fortunate enough to have several big-name stars training at his first gym, Astro's, in San Gabriel. Among them were Rory Leidelmeyer, Jon Aranita, Lonnie "Hams" Teper, Dennis Everly, Issac Curtis, and Derrick Cook. From the early to mid-1980s Astro's was the mecca of bodybuilding in Southern California's San Gabriel Valley.

Combining his newfound wisdom with his real life and aided by best buddy and training partner Bob Crowder, Cuevas slowly began to pack on the muscle he longed for. "By that

Photos courtesy of Steve Cuevas.

Steve Cuevas.

point I was already a big fan of Arnold Schwarzenegger and Robby Robinson, so working out along with some of the more recognizable names in bodybuilding added to my ambition to achieve my ultimate physique."

A lifetime drug-free lifter, Cuevas already weighed 200 pounds—at 20 years old—before he was even aware that anabolic steroids existed. "I never had a big desire to get really huge," he recalled. "My main goal was to achieve the most symmetrical, aesthetic physique I could, and steroids weren't the answer to getting that look. I had gone from 125 pounds to 200, and, even though I realized it would take extreme dedication, I was fully confident I could pack on another 20 pounds or so without ever touching a drug.

"However, perhaps even more important to me was the moral factor involved," he noted. His family—in addition to his parents, John and Terry, Cuevas has an older brother, Jeff, and two younger sisters, Gina and Marilyn— is very important to him. "Not only would it greatly disappoint my family and close friends if I took steroids, but the person I would let down the most would be myself. I have noth-

ing against other people taking anabolics if that's their choice, but it's just not me."

Along with his size and physique, Cuevas's strength improved annually, leading to lifts of 500 for 8 reps in the squat, 550 for 8 in the deadlift, and 365 for 6 in the bench. At a top weight of 227, Steve has amassed $27^1/_2$-inch thighs and 19-inch arms.

At World Gym, Pasadena, where he works as a personal trainer and hones his bod—he also works out and trains clients at Gold's Gym, Hollywood—he picked up the moniker "Hispanic Hercules" when a sleek, albeit small and smooth, reporter from *Ironman* magazine was stunned by his physique. I mean, hair, muscles, and veins were flowing all over the place, with thighs and hamstrings that reminded me of the world-class thoroughbred John Henry.

Although he's been noted for great musculature since the late 1980s, Cuevas didn't put on posing trunks until 1994, when he entered the ABCC Natural Nationals. The contest was held in Victorville, California, which happens to be the current hometown of Cuevas's parents.

Ron Harris, *Ironman* columnist and associate producer for the American Sports Network, which showcases bodybuilding and fitness on ESPN and ESPN2, persuaded the reserved 27-year-old Cuevas to enter the show. "I really never had an interest in competing," Cuevas said, "but after talking with Ron, I decided to experience the competition side of the sport."

Wise choice. At a weight of 184, Cuevas muscled his way to both the Tall and the Overall crowns. How good was his condition? According to a contest report that appeared in *Natural Bodybuilding*, Cuevas was "so cut he was almost bleeding." His parents, however, decided to pass on watching their son hit his poses live, choosing instead to watch the Junior Welterweight championship on TV, in which Julio Caesar Chavez's boxing opponent, Meldrick Taylor, got more cut than Cuevas while losing his battle for the title.

I was the next person to jump on Cuevas's back about competition, urging the muscle-bound lad of Mexican, Indian, and English ancestry to enter our Southern California

into my training," Cuevas said. "In the past I didn't need to do that to look sharp, but with the muscle I had gained in two years, cardio work would have made a big difference."

After finishing fifth in the '97 show, Cuevas dropped 3 to 4 pounds of water en route to taking the Tall Class two weeks later at Denny Kakos's ABA Natural World Championships, which were held a few blocks from World Gym. In that one Steve held his own against the supershredded B.J. Quinn, winner of the Middleweight class at the Ironman Naturally and the Overall champ at the NWC.

These days Cuevas, who has to slim down during certain periods of the year to accommodate his modeling and acting ambitions, spends more time in the aerobics room than Marvelous Mary Wong, a fitness fanatic who holds the gym's treadmill record of six hours in one day.

"I hope to get more into acting in the near future," said Cuevas. "I had a part last summer

Ironman Naturally Championships in 1995. I assured him of victory; he placed a disappointing fourth in the Light Heavyweight class, which saw Harris finish second and Karl List take first (as well as the Overall).

The only person more crushed than Cuevas was me, since my crystal ball looked clouded. Steve, what the heck happened?

"I made a mistake with my dieting," he said. "About a week before the contest I weighed 195 and felt I was in my best condition ever. I was really happy with my preparation at that point. But I panicked and overdieted, and by the time I hit the stage, I had dropped more than 10 pounds. Even though I was hard, I was way too flat."

Let's move forward two years. After more haranguing from yours truly (Cuevas set an NPC record by backing out of 17 contests in the next 23 months), he finally agreed to give the Ironman Naturally another shot.

This time his mistake wasn't coming in too flat, it was showing up too fat. "I was taking in too much sodium and didn't listen when my nutritionist at the gym told me I should incorporate some cardiovascular work

Never set limits on what you believe can be achieved naturally.

playing a hunk named Christian in the PBS television series 'A Question of Citizenship,' where I weighed 220, but in a couple of recent Vallejo weight belt commercials I got down to 195 for a more athletic look."

As far as training goes, Cuevas has some standard advice for the natural athlete. "First of all, never set limits on what you believe can be achieved naturally," he said. "To set realistic goals, though, you must be willing to be very patient, as it takes a lot longer to build mature muscle naturally.

"I normally train with a three-on/one-off, two-on/one-off regimen in the off-season, and I use a three-day bodypart split. On Day 1, I work chest, shoulders, triceps, calves, and abs. On Day 2 I hit quads, hamstrings, and lower back. For Day 3, I do back, traps, biceps, abs, and calves. Currently I'm doing cardio on a daily basis, but that depends on what I have going on careerwise. I know it sounds like I'm hitting way too many bodyparts per day, but because I limit my sets, I never spend more than one hour with the weights. I do 8 to 10 sets for large muscle groups and 6 to 8 for smaller bodyparts.

"I lift moderate weight, with fairly high reps, and I don't rest much between sets. About every three weeks or so I'll go heavier and cut the reps back to 6 to 8.

"I eat six to seven meals per day, with a ratio of about 50 percent protein, 35 percent carbs, and 15 percent fat. For contest training the ratio stays the same, but I drop my calories a bit and add cardio. I also add a few sets for most of my bodyparts."

As if he weren't busy enough with his Sculpted and Fit Physiques personal training business and budding acting and modeling career, Cuevas still finds time to serve as head coach of the Alhambra Dolphins Youth Swim Team, a group of competitive athletes who range in age from 6 to 17.

"I swam for the Rosemead club swim team when I was a youth," he said, "and I continued to compete at the high school level. An opportunity came up six years ago to be a head coach; I started at the YMCA in Alhambra and got the Dolphin job three years ago. I took the position because I like working with kids,

athletics, and building a team spirit that leads to camaraderie and values."

If the youngsters can build those components as successfully as Cuevas has built his body, they'll all end up in the winner's circle—in and out of a pool.

CUEVAS'S DIET AND NUTRITION

Meal 1
    8 egg whites scrambled in Pam cooking
        spray
    1 cup oatmeal mixed with 1 tablespoon
        essential fatty acids
    5 capsules glutamine
    5 capsules branched chain amino acids
        (BCCAS)

Meal 2
    3 scoops whey protein
    2 jars sweet potato baby food
    1 teaspoon essential fatty acids
    1 caplet fat burner

Meal 3
    8 ounces broiled top round steak
    1 medium baked potato
    $1/2$ cup cooked broccoli

Meal 4
    2 medium broiled chicken breasts
    1 cup oatmeal mixed with 1 teaspoon
        essential fatty acids
    3 ounces raw baby carrots
    Small green salad with low-calorie
        dressing

Meal 5 (Preworkout)
    8 ounces cooked turkey breast
    1 cup oatmeal mixed with 1 teaspoon
        essential fatty acids
    1 caplet fat burner
    2 scoops creatine monohydrate

Meal 6 (Postworkout)
    $2^{1}/2$ scoops whey protein
    $1^{1}/2$ scoops carb powder
    1 scoop creatine monohydrate
    5 capsules glutamine

Meal 7

    8 ounces cooked turkey breast
    1 small baked potato
    $^1/_2$ cup cooked broccoli
    5 capsules BCCAS
    1 tablespoon peanut butter

STEVE CUEVAS'S SHAPE-AND-MASS-BUILDING TRAINING

Day 1: Chest, Shoulders, Triceps, Calves, and Abs

Chest

Bench presses	3 × 6–15
Incline dumbbell presses	2 × 8–12
Flat-bench dumbbell flyes	2 × 8–12
Cable crossovers	2 × 10–12

Shoulders

Barbell presses	3 × 8–12
Seated lateral raises	3 × 8–12
One-arm bent-over laterals	3 × 8–15

Triceps

Seated EZ-curl bar extensions	3 × 8–15
Reverse-grip pushdowns	3 × 10–20
Bench dips	3 × 12–15

Calves

Machine donkey calf raises	3 × 12–25
Seated calf raises	3 × 12–20
Standing calf raises	3 × 12–20

Abs

Incline kneeups	3 × 15–25
Decline crunches	3 × 20–25

Day 2: Quads, Hamstrings, and Lower Back

Quads

Leg presses	3 × 8–15
Reverse hack squats	3 × 10–20
Leg extensions	3 × 10–15
Smith-machine lunges	3 × 15–20

Hamstrings and Lower Back

Seated leg curls	3 × 10–20
Lying leg curls	3 × 10–20
Stiff-legged deadlifts	3 × 10–16
Hyperextensions	3 × 15–20

Day 3: Back, Traps, Biceps, Abs, and Calves

Back

Pulldowns	3 × 8–15
Reverse-grip bent-over rows	3 × 8–15
Supported T-bar rows	2 × 8–12
Seated cable rows	2 × 8–12

Traps

Dumbbell shrugs	2 × 10–15
Upright rows	2 × 12–15

Biceps

Barbell curls	3 × 8–15
Seated dumbbell curls	2 × 8–12
Cable preacher curls	2 × 8–12

Abs

Incline reverse crunches	3 × 12–20
Machine crunches	3 × 15–20

Calves

Leg press calf raises	3 × 10–15
Seated calf raises	3 × 10–15
Machine donkey calf raises	3 × 10–15

ALL-NATURAL TRAINING TIPS

To be the best natural bodybuilder you can be, keep the following in mind:

1. Never set limits on what you can achieve naturally.
2. Never stop learning and experimenting.
3. Be patient. Understand that a lot of little improvements add up to great progress.
4. Be consistent and dedicated; maintain a positive outlook.

Here are some ideas to help you get the most out of your training for specific bodyparts.

Biceps

If you want to develop the front of your arms to the best of your genetic potential, you have to master the bottom, or beginning, portion of the curling motion. That's where a lot of people minimize the effectiveness of their biceps training. For instance, on barbell and dumbbell curls, never move your elbow or upper arm away from your torso. (If you find yourself doing that, your lower biceps are disproportionately weak compared to your upper biceps.) If, say, you move your elbows forward, your lower biceps won't be stimulated as much as the rest of the muscle, which over time will lead to unimpressive lower-biceps development. If that's your problem, cut back on the poundages and master the movement.

Also, do preacher curls and other exercises that fully stretch your biceps. That, along with keeping your upper arms stationary, will lead you to the massive arms you desire.

Triceps

For me the difference between a great triceps workout and a good or mediocre one has always been my ability to concentrate and really lock in and feel the triceps working hard through every inch of every rep. I guess it's the mind/muscle link working. Whatever the exercise, I try to feel the entire muscle bearing the weight and/or stretching on the complete negative portion of the movement, and then I accelerate slightly into the contraction.

I have to admit that I'm a little obsessed with contracting my triceps, holding it for about a second and squeezing harder and harder on each successive rep. Sometimes I actually feel the muscle might tear through the skin; however, that style of training has brought me the deep separations, striations, and size every bodybuilder wants to achieve.

Delts

I'll be the first to admit that with my naturally broad shoulders and background in swimming I didn't have to put in a lot of special effort to bring my shoulders into proportion with the rest of my physique. Based on my experience as well as conversations I've had with lots of successful bodybuilders, it seems the ticket to cannonball delts is as simple as one, two, three.

1. There's strength in the basics. As with most other bodyparts, using heavier weights leads to bigger muscles. Focus on pressing movements—performed with barbells, dumbbells, and machines—to improve your strength.
2. Variety always works—and that holds for all your bodyparts. Variety will help shock your muscles out of complacency and into new growth. You can accomplish that by changing your exercises, order of exercises, set-and-rep schemes, rest between sets, and other training factors.
3. Blood means growth. The chances are great that if you get a good pump in your deltoids and back it up with sound nutrition and plenty of rest and recuperation, they'll grow. If you aren't getting that satisfying flushing of blood in your shoulders, check out the following factors:
   - Are you eating the proper diet and getting enough rest before your workout?
   - Are you using mediocre or bad form on your exercises?
   - Are you focusing on your muscles during your sets?

Quads

As far as I'm concerned, quad training is a different animal from any other bodypart training. If your quads are the least bit stubborn or weak, you must—and I emphasize must—be able to bring your concentration, intensity, and pain threshold to levels that are beyond anything you've ever experienced before. Anyone who's achieved that will know what I'm talking about. No special exercises or form tips are as important as that. Just leave your ego at the door and get to work.

Hamstrings

When I train hamstrings, I think of them as big biceps that I'm just pumping with blood with every rep. That visualization motivates me and gives me a great feeling in my hams. On lying leg curls I use a special performance style that has helped make hams my best bodypart. When I start the movement, the bottom two-thirds of my quads are off the pad, and I stay that way throughout the rep. In fact, I might lift my quads even higher at the top to really hammer that contraction, and on the negative I stop about 30 degrees before my legs are straight so I don't lose tension in the target muscles. That might seem like a short range of motion, but the contraction you'll get in your hamstrings yields sensational results. You can also try it on seated leg curls and other hamstring exercises.

Abs

After I did my first contest, I realized that all those years of doing superhigh reps of 50 to 100 per set with little weight had given me a small waist that looked good on the beach but not the eye-popping muscle bellies you need for the competitive stage. So I added a significant amount of resistance to all my ab exercises and brought my sets down to a maximum of 25 reps. I emphasized the contraction almost to the point of cramping on every rep and felt a gnawing burn at the end of every set. As a result, at my next competition I had eye-popping abdominals.

Calves

I believe the most important aspect of calf training is to get a wide range of motion. Sure, some bodybuilders, thanks to genetics, have big calves no matter what they do. If yours are weak, as mine were years ago, you must be able to go heavy—using three to five times your bodyweight, depending on the exercise—performing 15 to 20 reps per set and using a complete range of motion to get them to grow. Train them four to six times a week for 12 to 15 sets per workout, and I guarantee you'll get results.

Chapter 7

SCIENTIFIC BODYBUILDING
BUILD BIG MUSCLES FAST

BY MICHAEL GÜNDILL

The most effective muscle-building protocol combines anabolic hormones and training. Pro bodybuilders are walking proof of that fact. They manipulate the levels of their muscle-building hormones artificially with drugs, and they train to enhance the effects of those hormones, creating a powerful synergy. Natural bodybuilders can train, but by definition they don't use any drugs. Does that condemn them to staying small? No!

For every bodybuilding drug there's a corresponding hormone that's naturally produced in your body. It's up to you to find a way to increase the secretion of your natural hormones. For each of those hormones there are corresponding receptors in your muscles that mediate their anabolic effects. It's up to you to find a way to upregulate those receptors and thereby persuade your body to release each hormone at specific times, and training is the tool you will use.

The purpose of the following training program is twofold: to naturally increase the levels of powerful anabolic hormones and to simultaneously upregulate their corresponding muscle receptors to get the most out of those hormones.

KNOW WHAT YOU'RE DOING

Most training programs are based on custom and/or what the trainee finds the most fun to do. They have no scientific basis. That's appropriate for recreational bodybuilders, but what if your goal is to get the most out of each workout while still remaining drug-free?

When drug users want bigger arms, they train their biceps and triceps and artificially increase the levels of some specific anabolic hormones. Instead of taking drugs, you can ask your body to naturally increase the secretion of those anabolic hormones. It's not as quick and easy as taking drugs, but it's legal and relatively safe.

As you can imagine, not just any kind of training will manipulate hormones in an optimal fashion. There's no room for guessing.

Unfortunately, many training programs are hormonally incoherent. For example, they increase your testosterone level while reducing the number of testosterone receptors on your muscles. That's not the way to create a synergy between your training and your hormones.

To promote the highest anabolic hormone level possible without taking drugs, you're going to enhance the sensitivity of those hormones on specific target muscles.

PUT SOME RATIONALITY INTO YOUR TRAINING

The following program is an example of how to put some logic into your training. It's by no means the only way to train. It's up to you to customize it to your specific needs instead of following it blindly, but first you have to understand why it makes sense. I didn't choose the training techniques, the exercises, and the rep schemes randomly or because they're fun. I chose them for their ability to stimulate both an anabolic hormone and its corresponding receptors on your muscles.

Each workout in the program targets a new hormone and its receptors, so you're constantly changing the way you train. A muscle responds well the first time to stimulation by an anabolic hormone. If you provide the same stimulation over and over, the muscles won't grow as well. A muscle will immunize itself against a repetitive stimulation, and it takes

time for your muscles to recover their previous sensitivity to a hormone.

That can make the program look complicated at first, but once you're used to it and you understand its logic, it will make sense. You'll also notice that you don't get the weekends off. Some people like to rest on Sunday. Good for them, but do your muscle fibers care whether it's a Sunday or a holiday? Not training on weekends is a practice based on custom, not rationality.

The hormone-manipulation training protocol is based on the following four-day cycle:

1. A pure negative workout, to stimulate local IGF-1 and FGF secretions and receptors.
2. A tension workout, to increase testosterone receptor levels and reduce the activity of the cortisol receptors.
3. A GH or insulin workout, to increase growth hormone secretion and GH receptors in the muscles and enhance their insulin sensitivity.
4. A rest day and then it starts all over again.

You end each workout with a single set of 100 repetitions, and every eight days you insert a testosterone-boosting quad workout.

Here's the schedule.

Workout 1: Testosterone-Boosting Quad Workout
Rest Day
Workout 2: Pure-Negative Back Workout
Workout 3: Tension Chest Workout
Workout 4: Insulin-Boosting Hamstring and Calf Workout
Rest Day
Workout 5: Pure-Negative Shoulder Workout
Workout 6: Tension Arm Workout
Workout 7: Testosterone-Boosting Quad Workout
Rest Day
Workout 8: GH-Boosting Back Workout
Workout 9: Pure-Negative Chest Workout

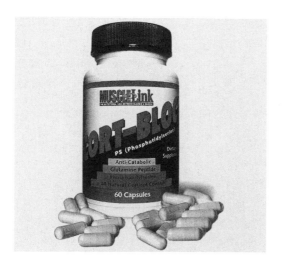

Workout 10: Tension Hamstring and
 Calf Workout
Rest Day
Workout 11: Insulin-Boosting
 Shoulder Workout
Workout 12: Pure-Negative Arm
 Workout
Workout 13: Testosterone-Boosting
 Quad Workout
Rest Day
Workout 14: Tension Back Workout
Workout 15: GH-Boosting Chest
 Workout
Workout 16: Pure-Negative Hamstring
 and Calf Workout
Rest Day
Workout 17: Tension Shoulder
 Workout
Workout 18: Insulin-Boosting Arm
 Workout

Start at Workout 1 again, but this time the GH-boosting workouts become insulin-boosting workouts and vice versa.

THE 100-REPETITION SET

You end each workout with a single set of 100 repetitions for a recovering bodypart in order to put some blood into recovering muscles and speed the healing process. It also hits muscle fibers that aren't stimulated by conventional workouts. Pick up a weight that allows you to do around 30 reps. That doesn't mean 30 is the maximum number of reps you can do but that to go beyond 30 you'd have to summon willpower. You should be able to reach 50 reps before stumbling. Rest 10 to 15 seconds and do 10 more reps, and so on until you reach 100. If you can do 110, next time either increase the weight slightly, reduce the rest time when you pass 50, or try to carry on for 15 reps instead of 10.

It's preferable to use a single-joint movement or a machine instead of free weights for this technique. Do leg extensions or leg presses instead of squats, and don't hesitate to choose a new exercise each time you do 100 reps on a specific bodypart. By the way, if a single set of

100 reps doesn't seem like enough, you're doing something wrong.

Here's the schedule for your 100-rep sets. After you work back, do a set of 100 reps for shoulders, alternating exercises for the three delts heads at consecutive back workouts. After chest do a set of 100 reps for biceps or triceps, alternating the two bodyparts on consecutive chest workouts. After hamstrings do a set of 100 reps for quads. After shoulders do a set of 100 reps for back. After arms do a set of 100 reps for chest.

These are the best exercises for 100-reps training:

Back: Kneeling stiff-arm cable
 pulldowns
Chest: Cable crossovers
Hamstrings: Seated leg curls
Calves: Donkey calf raises
Quads: Leg extensions
Anterior-delt heads: Cable front raises
Lateral-delt heads: Dumbbell or
 machine lateral raises
Posterior-delt heads: Seated bent-over
 dumbbell laterals
Biceps: Lying cable curls
Triceps: Standing cable pushdowns

Greg Blount.

TESTOSTERONE-BOOSTING WORKOUTS

Here are some tips for getting the most out of these sessions.

- Heavy partial squats will stimulate more testosterone than lighter full-range-of-motion squats. I'm not talking about a one- or two-inch-deep squat. Stop at just above parallel.
- Do as many reps as possible with the heaviest weight possible. The movement should be explosive. Don't slow down the negative portion of the rep too much, but don't go down so fast that you bounce back up at the bottom of the movement. Also, try forced reps to increase the intensity of the exercise.
- Repeat the testosterone-boosting workout every eight days. Don't forget it has long-lasting consequences. It will have a profound effect on your testosterone manufacture and release. It will force

your testes to increase their production of the hormone, and the release of the newly manufactured testosterone will last several days. On top of that, any high-intensity training will increase your testosterone level if you don't do too long a session. It won't be as potent as the testosterone-boosting workout, but it will enable you to extend the testosterone-boosting workout's effects.

- The testosterone-boosting workout should last less than 45 minutes. Remember, it's not truly a quad workout—although it should feel like one. It's just meant to increase testosterone secretion, and in this case more *isn't* better. If you keep going past 45 minutes, it will turn into a testosterone-*shrinking* workout.
- Take a day of rest after this workout. Your body isn't good at doing several different things at the same time. The testosterone-boosting effect will be stronger if your recovery ability isn't overwhelmed.
- Feel free to alternate squats with partial leg presses or hack squats as long as you put all you've got into the exercise.
- If you feel that the testosterone-boosting workout isn't enough for your quads— which it should be—you can add one quad exercise before the 100-rep set of leg curls.
- You can also alternate squats with partial deadlifts and do a normal workout for quads instead of hamstrings during that cycle (at workouts 4, 10, and 16). In that case the 100-rep set will be devoted to your hamstrings at those workouts.

Your testosterone workout should look like this:

Warm up

Half squats	1 × 20
Add weight	1 × 15
Add weight	1 × 10
Add weight	1 × 8
	+ 2 forced reps
Add weight	1 × 4–6
	+ 2 forced reps

Remove weight	1 × 12
	+ 8 forced
	rest/pause reps

THE NEGATIVE, IGF-1/FGF WORKOUTS

These are almost negative-only workouts. They're meant to force your muscles to secrete insulinlike growth factor 1 (IGF-1) and fibroblast growth factor (FGF), two powerful autocrine/paracrine anabolic hormones. The second exercise is designed to damage the fibers even further and facilitate the maximal upregulation of IGF-1 and FGF receptors.

Here are some important reminders for this workout.

- Warm up fully before starting the first exercise.
- The negative repetition should last around 10 seconds. That doesn't mean nine seconds in the top position and one while you're lowering the weight.
- If you feel the weight going down too quickly, don't hesitate to lighten the load—and that includes doing it during the exercise itself. The key point is to fight the weight with all you've got, not to impress others.
- Take a 5- to 10-second rest between negative repetitions. If you can move on quickly, there's something wrong with your intensity.
- Between sets, stretch, stretch, stretch.
- The second exercise is not supposed to be heavy. Move slowly. Stretch for two to four seconds in the bottom position. Then squeeze the muscle for two to four seconds at the top.
- Feel free to choose your own exercises or to change them frequently. The only rule is to end the workout with an exercise that provides a strong stretch.
- Don't train any bodyparts in this fashion too often. The program leaves 24 days between two negative workouts for the same bodypart.

Back

Negative-only wide-grip chins	3–4 × 6–10
Narrow-grip chins	3–4 × 10–15

Chest

Negative-only dips	3–4 × 6–10
Flat-bench or incline dumbbell flyes	3–4 × 12–20

Hamstring and calves

Negative-only leg curls	2–3 × 8–12
Stiff-legged deadlifts	2–3 × 15–20
Negative-only seated calf raises	2–3 × 8–12
Donkey calf raises	2–3 × 15–25

Quads (optional)

Negative-only one-leg presses	3–4 × 10–12
Hack squats	3–4 × 15–20

Shoulders

Negative-only Smith machine front presses	3–4 × 8–10
Bent-over laterals	3–4 × 12–15

Arms*

Negative-only curls	3–4 × 6–10
Negative-only lying EZ-curl bar triceps extensions	3–4 × 6–10
Preacher curls	3–4 × 10–15
One-arm behind-the-neck triceps extensions	3–4 × 12–15

*Train arms in a modified superset fashion: Do a biceps set, rest, then perform a triceps set. Rest, then repeat with a biceps set.

THE TENSION WORKOUTS

The objective of these sessions is twofold: to rapidly increase the number of androgen receptors on the trained muscles and to put cortisol receptors out of order. To achieve these goals, you must build up muscle tension without inducing too much fiber trauma.

This workout is the antithesis of the negative workout. You want to put tension on the positive part of the repetition while avoiding emphasizing the negative part. Furthermore, while a pure negative workout is meant to induce muscle trauma, the tension workout is designed to minimize it.

Understand that one type of workout isn't better than the other. Each stimulates muscle growth by different means. By using both, you prevent your muscles from getting used to one type of stimulation. You do more tension workouts than negative workouts because the tension workouts are less traumatic and require less recovery time.

Alternating the two workouts creates a synergy, as each type of training needs the other to work better.

Here are some important points regarding the tension workouts.

- The goal is to put as much tension as possible on the trained muscles. That implies training with heavy weights but with strict form only.
- Cheating transfers the tension from the muscles to the tendons, which is highly undesirable.

- Keep the target muscle under tension for as long as possible. So instead of counting reps, you're better off counting time under tension.
- Use a stop-and-go training tempo, taking three to six seconds on the way up, two seconds in the top position, two seconds on the way down, and two seconds at the bottom.
- Don't forget to stop the weight for two seconds at the bottom of the movement before starting the positive part of the rep. It makes the positive part of the movement much harder, forcing you to build up tension.
- Squeeze the muscle in the contracted position for at least two seconds.
- As you feel the weight getting heavier, slow down your rep speed even more instead of accelerating it. Remember, it's time under tension that matters here, not the number of reps you get. The point at which most people would stop the exercise is where you should dig in and give it your best.
- Even if the weight isn't moving much anymore, as long as you can produce muscle tension, keep on going.
- To increase the time under tension, it seems logical to choose the movements that offer the greatest range of motion possible. For example, one-arm dumbbell rows are better than T-bar rows. Training one side of your body at a time will help you concentrate better and so produce more tension. It's not always possible to train one side at a time, but do so whenever you can.
- Try not to traumatize the muscle fibers too much. Avoid explosive or bouncing movements. Doing set after set will prove traumatic as well. Look to reduce the number of sets and increase training intensity.
- Long workouts will induce the release of cortisol more than short ones. Keep your training intense but brief.
- Frequent workouts will put a burden on your recovery ability. To recover from

that burden, the body will release corti-sol. So avoid training too frequently.

Back

Machine pullovers	3–4 × 10–15
One-arm dumbbell rows	3–4 × 6–12
One-arm lat pulldowns	3–4 × 8–12

Chest

Flat-bench dumbbell presses	3–5 × 6–12
Dips	3–5 × 6–15

Hamstrings and Calves

Standing leg curls	3–4 × 10–15
Seated one-leg curls	3–4 × 6–12
Donkey calf raises	4–6 × 6–20

Quads (Optional)

One-leg presses	3–4 × 6–12
Hack squats	3–4 × 6–12
One-leg extensions	3–4 × 12–20

Shoulders

Machine presses	3–4 × 6–12
One-arm cable laterals or machine laterals	3–4 × 10–12
Bent-over dumbbell laterals	3–4 × 8–20

Arms*

Seated one-arm dumbbell curls	3–4 × 6–12
One-arm triceps extensions	3–4 × 6–12
One-arm machine curls	2–3 × 10–15
One-arm pushdowns	2–3 × 10–15

*Perform biceps and triceps exercises with modified supersets.

THE GH WORKOUT

The purpose of this workout is twofold: to increase GH receptors on the trained muscles and to boost GH secretion. You accomplish that by training in a postfatigue superset fashion.

- The first movement is a compound exercise. Use heavy weight with an explosive, dynamic movement.
- Resist on the way down. It's even better if you have your training partner push on the weight to make the negative part of the rep harder.
- Immediately superset with a lighter single-joint movement targeting the same muscles.
- You want to involve as much muscle mass as possible. In this case you avoid training one side of the body and then the other.
- During the second, lighter exercise go for muscle burn. Don't count reps. The workload should depend on how much burn you can stand. It's for a good cause: intense muscle burn is the strongest stimulator of GH release.
- Use a full range of motion on the single-joint movement. Reduce the range as your muscle gets tired in order to optimize the burning sensation.
- When pain is too intense, rest for 5 to 10 seconds, then resume the exercise.
- You can use quick movements in the second exercise, but to avoid injuries, try to keep the negative part of the rep under control.
- Only the combination of more muscle GH receptors plus a high secretion of GH will induce muscle growth. You won't get any anabolic GH effect if you don't combine the two factors.

Back
Superset

Weighted chinups	4–6 × 6–12
Kneeling stiff-arm pulldowns	4–6 × 15–25

Chest
Superset

Bench presses	4–6 × 6–12
Cable crossovers	4–6 × 15–25

Hamstrings
Superset

Stiff-legged deadlifts	3–5 × 6–12
Lying leg curls	3–5 × 15–25

Calves
Superset

Standing calf raises	3–5 × 6–12
Seated calf raises	3–5 × 15–25

Quads (Optional)
Superset
Hack squats · 4–6 × 6–12
Leg extensions · 4–6 × 15–25

Shoulders
Superset
Front presses · 4–6 × 6–12
Lateral raises* or bent-
over laterals · 4–6 × 15–25

Biceps**
Superset
Barbell curls · 3–5 × 6–12
Straight-bar cable curls · 3–4 × 15–25

Triceps**
Superset
Lying triceps extensions · 3–5 × 6–12
Pushdowns · 3–5 × 15–25

*Alternate the exercises at consecutive growth-hormone shoulder workouts.

**Feel free to use modified supersets for the biceps and triceps work. When you're done with a biceps superset, rest as you normally would, then do a triceps superset. Rest and repeat with a biceps superset, and so on.

THE INSULIN WORKOUT

The objective of this workout is to pump up the muscles to empty them of their glycogen and bring in as much blood as possible. Here are some tips to remember.

- High reps are desirable.
- Your training tempo should be fast. Reduce rest time to the bare minimum.
- Choose nontraumatic movement—for example, use cable and machine exercises instead of free weights.
- Reduce the range of motion to enhance the muscle pump and prevent the blood from leaving the muscles.
- Avoid training only one side of the body at a time.
- Eat high-carb foods right after the workout. Any training will reduce insulin levels, not elevate them.

Back
Wide-grip front lat
pulldowns · 5–6 × 12–20
Seated cable rows · 5–6 × 12–20

Chest
Decline-bench presses · 4–6 × 12–20
Pec deck flyes · 4–6 × 12–20

Hamstrings and Calves
Lying leg curls · 4–5 × 12–20
Seated leg curls · 4–5 × 12–20
Donkey calf raises · 5–6 × 15–30

Quads (Optional)
Leg presses · 5–6 × 15–25
Leg extensions · 5–6 × 15–25

Shoulders
Lateral raises · 4–5 × 12–20
Front presses · 3–5 × 12–20
Pec deck rear-delt flyes · 3–5 × 12–20

Arms*
Cable curls · 3–5 × 12–20
Pushdowns · 3–5 × 12–20
Lying cable curls · 3–5 × 15–25
Cable triceps extensions · 3–5 × 15–25

*Perform biceps and triceps exercises with modified supersets.

You can see that variety is key here. You use all the different anabolic techniques at your disposal to force your muscles to grow. Feel free to add even more variety. Use the program as a sample. You can change the exercises if you wish, as long as you respect the basic rules. Of course, the system will work even better if you follow a good nutrition and supplementation program.

HOW TO AMPLIFY YOUR MASS-BUILDING RESULTS FROM ENDOCRINE-PULSE TRAINING—OR ANY WEIGHT-TRAINING PROGRAM

The outlandish muscle size of drug-using physique competitors drives home a fact all bodybuilders should be aware of: Combining weight training with hormone manipulation

compounds: tribulus terrestris, androstene-dione, norandrostenedione, norandrostene-diol, and 5-androstenediol. Norandro derivatives have proven to be the most effective; however, one study showed that combining androstenedione with tribulus terrestris created an average gain of 7.4 pounds of lean mass in only 28 days.

IGF-1- and FGF-boosting workout

Heavy negatives can take a toll on your joints, so you may want to try a natural connective-tissue builder such as chondroitin and glucosamine sulfate. This combination was popularized by the book *The Arthritis Cure* by Jason Theodosakis, Barry Fox, Ph.D., and Brenda Adderly. A GH-boosting supplement can help drive up IGF-1 levels.

GH-boosting workout

A GH-booster supplement such as Pro-hGH may also help increase your levels of this hormone. This new effervescent supplement is getting rave reviews from young and old bodybuilders alike. Plus, it can help you burn more fat as you build muscle.

Tension workout

A phosphatidylserine supplement may help reduce cortisol levels, which will increase recovery and facilitate muscle growth. A study done by Thomas Fahey, Ph.D., of California State University, Chico, found that soy-based PS reduced blood cortisol levels after bodybuilding workouts by almost 30 percent. Cortisol is a stress hormone that can eat muscle tissue, a phenomenon bodybuilders, especially hardgainers, want to minimize at every opportunity.

Insulin-boosting workout

Studies indicate that an insulin surge after a workout is a prerequisite for forcing high-level nutrient uptake by the depleted muscle cells. This is known as the anabolic window of

creates explosive muscle growth, no doubt about it. With Endocrine-Pulse training, explained in the *Scientific Bodybuilding* series by Michael Gündill, you can manipulate your hormone levels in the gym—without drugs—and certain supplements can be invaluable for amplifying the anabolic effects of this training protocol. Here are some you may want to try with the corresponding Endocrine-Pulse workout they enhance.

Testosterone-boosting workout

To heighten testosterone release, you may want to try one or a combination of the following opportunity, an event you can't afford to waste. The key ingredients for optimizing this window are 50 grams of protein, 50 to 100 grams of simple carbohydrate, and 3 to 5 grams of creatine. For example, use three scoops of Muscle-Linc's Nitro Stak mixed in three cups of orange juice. This will give you more than 50 grams of protein, 70 grams of high-glycemic carbs, and 5 grams of creatine, which achieves better cell uptake due to the simple-carb shuttle. Nitro Stak's whey protein-and-creatine for-mula also includes nitrogen-retention com-pounds, such as KIC, that help preserve and build muscle tissue after you train.

Ideal supplements for hormone manipula-tion, as outlined by Endocrine-Pulse Training include the following Muscle-Linc products: 5-Androstenediol and 19-Norandro (testos-terone boosters), Flex Stak (joint protection), Pro-hGH (growth hormone stimulation), Cort-Bloc (cortisol suppression), and Nitro Stak (muscle-tissue building).

Barbell triceps extension.

Chapter 8

THE AMAZING MASS-BUILDING HARDGAINER SOLUTION

BY STEVE HOLMAN

Your metabolism races faster than a revving Testarosa, your wrists and ankles have the diameters of twigs from an undernourished sapling, and your muscle growth is about as fast as a snail on Quaaludes. In bodybuilding you're known as a hardgainer, but a better description would be genetically cursed. You believe you have about as much chance of hitting poses in front of a cheering crowd as Howard Stern has of becoming president of the Daughters of the American Revolution—even if he does look mighty fetching in a skirt and pantyhose. It's impossible for you to attain a competition-worthy physique, right? Not so fast, there, fellow hardgainer.

Allow me to revert to first person for a few paragraphs and regale you with my own story. It's important for you to know that I'm not some genetic Dorian Yates–type superfreak telling hardgainers how to train. That would be like Troy Aikman trying to teach a guy with no arms how to throw a football 50 yards.

I'm far from being gifted in the muscle-building department. Talk about genetically

cursed! My father weighed all of 115 pounds—no doubt after a big meal—when he married my mother, who weighed a whopping 95, fully clothed and holding a large purse. It was a union of two string-bean physiques: Barney Fife meets Olive Oyl. At 16, I was the spitting image of my rail of a father in his teenage years—OK, so I had him by about 5 pounds; I weighed in at just under 120—and at my most-muscular I looked like newsreel footage from the World War II concentration camps.

When you're that skinny in high school, you do one of three things: You turn into an introvert and get beaten up a lot, join the chess club and get beaten up a lot, or lift weights so the thought of beating you up crosses fewer people's minds.

Of course, I was still damn skinny all through high school, even with my intense weight-training sessions. I was 5'10", and my bodyweight hovered around 160 during my senior year. I'm sure many readers can identify with that plight, but even at 160 I had enough visible muscle on my frame to ward off the

Bench press.

Steve Cuevas.

majority of beatings. If bullies see a hint of sinew, they tend to look elsewhere for a victim.

I was the living embodiment of Jolly Roger, the skull-and-crossbones figure on pirate flags, when I entered college, which may account for my voracious thirst for bodybuilding knowledge. I knew it held the key to overcoming my physical inadequacies—if only I could determine the perfect training routine that would pack mass on my bamboo-shoot body.

At the University of Texas at Austin I hit the books hard, doing most of my research papers on muscle growth and the best way to trigger it. I combed the science libraries for hypertrophy-related studies and abstracts, and lo and behold, I actually uncovered a number of things that made efficient muscle building much easier, especially for hardgainers.

For example, I learned that the myotatic reflex occurs when a muscle is stretched and then forced to contract soon thereafter. The stretch puts the target muscle in an emergency-response mode, which can cause an inordinate number of muscle fibers to fire. In other words, you get more growth stimulation from

each rep when the myotatic reflex is engaged. If you use it correctly, this technique can cause you to leap-frog genetic growth limitations by

tricking the nervous system into believing it must grow in order to prevent severe trauma, such as muscle tears.

I took this knowledge into the gym and made some of the best gains of my life. My bodyweight eventually shot over the 200-pound mark, and I entered and won my very first bodybuilding contest. People were even accusing me of being an easygainer.

This metabolic shift out of the genetic trash bin didn't just magically happen, however. It took a lot of experimentation. While it's true that, once I identified and began using a stretch-position movement for each bodypart, my gains increased significantly, I also had to go back to my research and hone the other factors that contribute to muscle growth.

TRIGGERING HYPERTROPHY

According to Michael Wolf, Ph.D., the following changes are associated with increases in muscle size and strength:

1. The actin and myosin protein filaments increase in size.
2. The number of myofibrils increases.
3. The number of blood capillaries within the fiber may increase.
4. The amount of connective tissue within the muscle may increase.
5. The number of muscle fibers may increase.

If you train in the 7-to-12-rep range with heavy weights often enough, you stress the type-II, or fast-twitch, muscle fibers, which will positively affect the actin and myosin filaments and increase the number of myofibrils (points 1 and 2 above). Most bodybuilders know this is the appropriate mass-building rep range and use it at every workout, so there's no real insight for the hardgainer there; however, point 3—increasing the number of blood capillaries—holds some real muscle-building possibilities.

Forcing blood into the muscle and inducing a pump causes new capillaries to form in the target muscle, which increases the muscle's size. How much bigger does the muscle get?

It's hard to say because the percentage of increase may depend on genetics. Ah, but isn't this article about breaking through those barriers? Absolutely. So here are a couple of things that facilitate the pump and force more capillarization no matter what your genetics.

Carbohydrates

While dietary carbs are getting a bad rap these days because of their association with insulin and fat deposition, you, a hardgainer, shouldn't worry about that. Your blast-furnace metabolism won't allow for much fat storage, and any excess glycogen you can infuse into the muscles will help you attain a skin-stretching pump in the shortest time possible. Remember, with your limited recovery ability, you can't waste time and energy doing endless sets to get a pump that increases the number of capillaries. You have to blow up the muscle in a few sets and then get out of the gym so you can grow.

Try to eat some carbohydrates at every meal, which means six times a day, along with your feedings of 30 to 40 grams of protein. Don't be afraid of taking in some fat at a few of your meals either. New research says that fat can help bolster testosterone production, which in turn can help you build muscle.

Crossovers.   Ron Harris.

Supersets

Combining two exercises for the same muscle will do tremendous things for growth. Not only will it help you achieve a mind-blowing pump fast, spurring capillary generation, but new research suggests that it can also lower the pH of the blood and stimulate growth hormone release. As European researcher Michael Gündhill wrote in "The Science of Supersetting," in the August '97 *Ironman*, "Research shows that this type of training not only increases GH levels, but it also increases GH receptors located on the trained muscles." This is truly exciting research. Go for the burn and you'll definitely pack on mass faster.

CONNECTIVE TISSUE AND FIBER SPLITTING

How do you increase the amount of connective tissue and/or perhaps increase the number of muscle fibers?

Connective-tissue generation has to do with using heavy weights, so relying on the big compound movements—squats, deadlifts, and rows—is key. Most hardgainers know that those exercises are best for mass stimulation, so they use them as the core of their workouts. In addition, stretch-position movements, such as sissy squats for quads and stiff-legged deadlifts for hamstrings, help increase connective tissue because they elongate the target muscle, creating more stress at the origin and insertion points.

As for increasing the number of muscle fibers, or hyperplasia, this is still a controversial topic. Some researchers believe it is a fantasy. Nevertheless, one animal study showed that muscle-fiber hyperplasia does occur as a result of—get ready—"stretch overload" (Antonio, J., and Gonyea, W.J. [1993]. Skeletal muscle fiber hyperplasia. *Medicine and Science in Sports and Exercise.* 25:1333–45). The possibility of even small increases in the number of fast-twitch fibers is reason enough to use stretch-position movements. Another reason is fascial stretching.

LESS CONSTRICTION, MORE GROWTH

Stretch-position movements stretch the fascia, or the membrane that encases the muscle fibers. A looser encasement can mean there's more freedom for a muscle to grow because there's less fiber constriction. A good example of this constriction/slow-growth connection is the former Chinese tradition of binding girls' feet. Because tiny feet were considered attractive in the Chinese culture, wealthy families had their daughters' feet tightly bound for years at a time so that growth would be stunted—and it worked, although it was extremely painful. Fascia can act in the same constricting manner and restrict a muscle's growth, according to a number of trainers and researchers, one of whom is John Parrillo.

Parrillo suggests performing separate fascial-stretching sessions to facilitate faster muscle growth, but when you incorporate stretch-position movements into your routine, you don't need special sessions. The stretch-position movements do a good job of elongating the target muscles to the maximum and thus produce a fairly severe fascial stretch with each rep. To enhance the effect, you can hold the stretch-position of your last rep on these exercises for 5 to 10 seconds; however, don't do this on every rep or you diffuse the myotatic reflex.

UNLEASH NEW SIZE

One of the catch-22s of hardgainer training is that to build a muscle to extraordinary levels, you must train it from a number of angles, but when you do that, you can overstress your recovery ability and overtrain, which slows or halts growth. The bottom line is, if you want tremendous muscle growth in every bodypart, you have to use multi-angular training without overtraining. Of course, many experts will tell you that all you need is one exercise per bodypart to get maximum development, but don't be fooled. It's just not that simple. If you follow that logic, you'll be using the hard-

Deadlift—start.

Deadlift—finish.

gainer excuse for the rest of your days. The reality is that only certain fibers, those that have the best leverage during a particular exercise, will grow as a result of your doing that exercise, so you have to make sure the fibers contract in a variety of positions if you want to maximize the number of fibers that get total growth stimulation.

To help you understand the need for more than one exercise per bodypart, here's a quote from Jaci VanHeest, renowned exercise physiologist at the United States Olympic Training Center in Colorado Springs, Colorado.

Muscles contract when tiny levers on myosin, a muscle protein, fit into grooves on actin, another protein, and push it forward exactly like a ratchet wrench. But myosin can latch onto actin in any of several positions, not all of them ideal. Only when the myosin heads are in the right register can the muscle have the optimal

tension. But optimizing every actin-myosin pairing is less an achievable goal than a Platonic ideal.

Essentially, that means almost every exercise optimizes a different configuration of actin-myosin pairings. While there's some overlap, you have to exercise a muscle in a number of positions to optimize as many of the actin-myosin pairings as possible.

After reading the above, you may think that you, the hardgainer with limited recovery ability, are doomed. You can't possibly train every muscle from a variety of angles without smashing headfirst into the overtraining wall. Ah, but what if you used different exercises at different workouts to cover all the angles—say, in two workouts rather than trying to do all angles at one session? You would leap over your so-called genetic barriers and grow beyond your wildest imagination.

THE ULTIMATE HARDGAINER ROUTINE

To construct the Ultimate Hardgainer Routine, we must first identify what "multi-angular training" means. Each muscle essentially has three positions, or angles, you should strive to train in order to optimize as many actin-myosin pairings as possible: midrange, stretch, and contracted. Many of you will recognize these as positions of flexion. For those of you unfamiliar with POF, here's a quick example using triceps.

> You train the midrange position with close-grip bench presses or lying extensions.
> You train the stretch position with overhead extensions—upper arms next to your head.
> You train the contracted position with kickbacks—upper arms behind the torso for a maximum contraction.

Note that you train three different points along the arc of flexion—from the overhead position to the hands-over-the-chest position to the behind-the-torso position.

This arc isn't as simple to define for some bodyparts, such as quads, but you can still put every exercise into one of those categories. Squats, leg presses, and hack squats are midrange movements because they do not completely stretch or fully contract the quads and they use synergy from other muscles to help the quads perform work; a sissy squat is a stretch-position movement for quads because the torso and thighs are on the same plane, and when the hamstrings and calves meet, the quads are completely stretched; and leg extensions are the contracted-position movement because the torso and thighs are at almost 90 degrees to each other and there is resistance in the contracted, or knees-locked, position.

One last point about triggering inordinate muscle growth. Michael Gündill, a European researcher, has explained how muscle soreness can enhance hypertrophy. His conclusion is that pure-negative sets can be very effective at inducing an anabolic environment but should be used infrequently to avoid too much mus-

cle damage. You may want to add a negative set here and there to this routine every so often. I highly recommend it. Changing the stress is one way to keep growth moving upward. Just don't get carried away with this technique, or you'll undoubtedly overtrain.

Give the Ultimate Hardgainer Routine a fair trial, make adjustments where necessary, and you may be surprised at just how much easier it is to put on muscle. In fact, after you add slabs of new muscle to every bodypart, you may even be accused of being an easy-gainer—by the other four finalists standing on stage with you waiting for the winner's name to be called.

THE ULTIMATE HARDGAINER ROUTINE

Monday
Quads and hamstrings

Squats or leg presses*	2 × 7–10
Leg extensions	1 × 7–10

Hamstrings

Leg curls*	2 × 7–10

Chest

Bench presses*	2 × 7–10
Crossovers	1 × 7–10

Delts

Dumbbell presses*	2 × 7–10
Lateral raises	1 × 7–10

Lats

Front pulldowns*	2 × 7–10
Stiff-arm pulldowns	1 × 7–10

Midback

Behind-the-neck pulldowns*	2 × 7–10
Forward-lean shrugs	1 × 7–10

*Do 1 or 2 light warm-up sets with 50 to 70 percent of your work-set weight prior to your work sets.

Wednesday
Triceps

Lying extensions*	2 × 7–10
Superset	
Overhead extensions	2 × 5–8
Kickbacks	2 × 5–8

Squat.

Biceps

Barbell curls*	2 × 7–10
Superset	
Incline curls	2 × 5–8
Spider curls	2 × 5–8

Calves

Superset	
Donkey calf raises or	
leg press calf raises*	2 × 10–15
Standing calf raises	2 × 10–15
Seated calf raises	2 × 12–20

Abdominals

Incline kneeups	2 × 7–10
Full-range crunches or	
ab bench crunch pulls	2 × 7–10

*Do 1 or 2 light warm-up sets with 50 to 70 percent of your work-set weight prior to your work sets.

Friday

Quad superset

Sissy squats	2 × 5–8
Squats or leg presses	2 × 5–8

Hamstrings drop set*

Stiff-legged deadlifts	2 × 5–8

Chest superset

Flat-bench flyes	2 × 5–8
Bench presses	2 × 5–8

Delt superset

One-arm incline laterals	2 × 5–8
One-arm dumbbell	
presses	2 × 5–8

Lat superset

Dumbbell pullovers	2 × 5–8
Front pulldowns	2 × 5–8

Midback drop set*

Forward-lean shrugs	2 × 5–8

Note: Do 1 light warm-up set of each exercise before doing your superset. Also, stop your stretch-exercise work set a few reps short of failure, but push the second exercise till you can't get another rep in perfect form.

*To perform a drop set, do 1 set to failure, then quickly reduce the weight and perform another set to failure.

WHY THIS ROUTINE PACKS ON MASS

1. Each workout takes about one hour—with fewer than 20 work sets—which is perfect for the hardgainer's limited recovery ability. You can keep your intensity high without burning out.

2. There's a day of rest between workouts and then two days' rest at the end of the cycle, which facilitates systemic recovery.

3. The big compound movements are at the core of each workout—the first exercise for each bodypart on Monday and Wednesday and the second exercise in the supersets on Friday. They train the mass of the target muscle and also help develop tendon and ligament size and strength.

4. The use of supersets and drop sets helps develop more capillaries in the target muscle and also can increase growth hormone release. Plus, by using stretch-position movements as the first exercise in a superset, you kick the muscles into hypercontraction, which activates extreme fiber recruitment during the second exercise in the superset.

5. The use of stretch-position movements on Wednesday and Friday helps stretch the fascia to allow for more muscle growth, develops tendon and ligament size and strength, and produces more fiber recruitment through neurological stimulation and by placing the muscle in an emergency-response mode. Stretch overload may also cause hyperplasia, or fiber splitting, which can increase the growth potential of a muscle.

6. The rep ranges listed are ideal for activating type-II muscle fibers, which are the fibers with the most growth potential.

7. By training each muscle from three distinct angles, or positions—midrange,

stretch, and contracted—you optimize as many actin-myosin pairings as possible and therefore stimulate complete development in every target muscle.

8. Arms get only one direct hit a week, which prevents overtraining them. Remember, you get indirect arm work from all the pressing, rowing, and pulling at your other two workouts.

STRETCH YOUR GAINS

Using stretch-position movements has a number of hypertrophic benefits, including the following:

1. Loosens fascial constriction to facilitate more fiber growth.
2. Develops tendon and ligament size and strength.
3. Increases neuromuscular efficiency for better fiber recruitment.
4. May stimulate hyperplasia, or fiber splitting (this is still debatable from a scientific standpoint).

Here's a list of the best stretch-position exercises for each bodypart:

Quads: Sissy squats

Hamstrings: Stiff-legged deadlifts

Calves: Donkey calf raises or leg press calf raises

Chest: Flyes

Delts: One-arm incline laterals

Lats: Pullovers

Midback: Close-grip cable rows

Biceps: Incline curls

Triceps: Overhead extensions

Abdominals: Full-range crunches

Incorporating these exercises into your routine—using correct form—at least once a week can significantly increase muscle growth.

Steve Holman.

Skip La Cour.

Chapter 9

THINKING BIG

BY SKIP LA COUR

Hitting a plateau, otherwise known as having your training progress come to a screeching halt, is probably one of the most feared and frustrating phenomena a bodybuilder can experience. No one wants to work extremely hard at something and show no signs of improvement. That's especially true when it comes to such a demanding lifestyle as bodybuilding.

Having your training stagnate will surely lead to frustration—a feeling that undercuts the fulfillment you hope to enjoy from body-building. Mounting frustration will eventually overwhelm you. Becoming overwhelmed is the primary reason many lifters stop training altogether.

Unfortunately, too many bodybuilders quit due to the frustration caused by what they perceive as a lack of progress. With that disempowering perception, they can only muster a halfhearted effort at best as a way of protecting themselves from experiencing the pain. That situation occurs whether or not the person realizes what is happening. That's usu-

ally the time you start hearing some natural bodybuilders complain about their poor genetics or their hardgainer status, or when they become convinced that what they had hoped to accomplish with their physiques is impossible because they don't use drugs.

Plateaus are definitely to be avoided, and in my opinion, they can be. Reexamine how you currently define a plateau, and start thinking big!

Sometimes what we perceive as plateaus are actually the following pitfalls in our thinking.

- We are not being persistent enough in finding the answers to training challenges that, if discovered, will propel us to higher levels of development.
- We really are getting results—they just aren't visible to us quite yet.
- We compare ourselves unrealistically and/or unfairly to other bodybuilders.
- We are not being creative enough to uncover new, exciting, and unique ways

to enjoy the entire spectrum of fulfillment bodybuilding has to offer.

- We don't realize we are growing in ways that are more important than physical growth.

BE PERSISTENT TO FIND BETTER STRATEGIES

Bodybuilders say to me such things as, "I just can't figure out how to get my shoulders to grow! I've tried so many different routines and nothing seems to work."

"Exactly how many is so many?" I ask them. Normally, if they reply honestly, they have actually tried no more than three or four different routines.

There are obviously many more than just three or four ways to train shoulders. You could train them once a week or twice. You could even train them once every other week.

Greg Blount.

You could train them very heavily, moderately, or lightly. You could put extra focus on the negative movement. You could perform a high number of repetitions or very few. You could train with a partner or alone. You could have a person spot you or use only as much weight as you can handle yourself. You could train in the morning, when your natural growth hormone level is supposed to be at its highest, or later, when your closest rival is there to motivate you to take your training to the next level. You could train shoulders after setting a contest date for one year from now or after initiating a shoulder-building contest with your buddies. You could train while on a high-protein, moderate-protein, or low-protein diet. You could train with different amounts of carbohydrates in your system or with the many different nutritional supplements available today. Then you could switch, mix up, and rotate every single one of those variables for different periods of time.

Would each of the factors lead to different results in the development of your shoulders? You bet they would! You and I would never stop trying after only three or four different routines and then blame our lack of improvement on a training plateau, would we? As a natural bodybuilder you will probably mature at an older age (in your mid-30s or older). Don't just assume you'll become outstanding when that time rolls around if you aren't persistent enough to put your time, effort, and intelligence into your training today.

YOU MAY BE GETTING RESULTS WITHOUT EVEN REALIZING IT

Stop and think about your situation for a moment. Can your progress ever really stop if you're consistently putting forth your best effort? If you're training with regularity and intensity and supporting that training with sound nutritional practices, you can rest assured you're not really stagnant—regardless of what you may think. (If you're not, then you're obviously not at a plateau.) Often, you're improving even when you aren't aware of it.

One of my favorite illustrations of this comes from motivational speaker Zig Ziglar. He talks about a man who goes to an old-fashioned well to pump some drinking water. The man pushes the pump's lever over and over again and is seemingly making no progress.

The man is indeed making progress, however. It just isn't visible to him at the time. His pumping is creating suction deep in the underground pipes and is slowly siphoning the water to the surface. If he gets discouraged and stops pumping, the water will fall back down—and he'll have to start all over again. If he is persistent, the man will eventually see results from his efforts. At that point he'll no longer need to pump as hard because now only a little force will produce enough water to equal 10 times the effort he gave at the beginning.

Sometimes it feels as though you're putting 10 times more effort into your train-

ing than you seem to be getting back in improvements. If you're persistent, you'll enjoy bodybuilding benefits that could be 10 times greater than the effort you invest—just like the man in the example.

Another problem may be that you see yourself too often to truly appreciate your progress. Have you ever had a friend who hasn't seen you in a while tell you how muscular you've gotten? That friend's perception is probably a little more accurate than yours. We often become our own worst enemies. The same drive that motivates us to become our very best sometimes makes us too tough on ourselves.

If you keep pressing yourself to train harder and learn more, you never know when a big payoff in significant muscle mass will occur. One thing is certain, however. You won't see results if you stop giving 100 percent of your effort, get frustrated, or quit.

DON'T MAKE UNFAIR COMPARISONS

Sometimes we're winning but feel as though we're losing. I had a training partner who was no better than average when we first began working out together. Within months his physique dramatically improved and the amount of weight he tackled increased by at least 30 percent.

He was initially ecstatic about his progress and set the ambitious goal of winning the drug-tested Musclemania Bodybuilding Championships later that year. Unfortunately, his excitement didn't last very long. His gains did not come as quickly as he expected, and he became discouraged. Although he had only been training for about three years—with only a small portion of that at a maximum intensity level—he wanted a great physique *now*.

"I get so down when I look in the magazines, Skip," he confessed. "I look at those guys, and the only thing I think is that I don't look like that."

He was being terribly unfair to himself by making such comparisons. The bodybuilders in the magazines more than likely have at least

twice as much training experience. In addition, most of their training has probably been as focused as his few intense months.

We no longer train together, as other things in his life now have a higher priority. He no longer dreams of winning a national show or being featured in an international magazine. Bodybuilding, which for a short time brought him so much pride, fulfillment, accomplishment, and optimism, is no longer an interest. He had been winning the game in a big way, in my opinion, but he felt as though he was losing.

ENJOY MORE OF THE EXCITEMENT BODYBUILDING HAS TO OFFER

The truth is you can never really plateau when it comes to bodybuilding because there are countless exciting facets of this complex lifestyle to enjoy. Here's a unique way to break through any plateau you feel you're experiencing: Fall in love with bodybuilding! Take your passion for the sport to a whole new level. Make it much more than a fun hobby or a passing interest.

"What do you mean, La Cour? I already love to train, eat a lot of protein, and read the magazines every month!" I know what you're thinking, but reducing this lifestyle/sport of bodybuilding to simply working out, eating right, and thumbing through its publications is like saying the Louvre has a few interesting paintings. You are robbing yourself of so much of the stimulation that's available for you to enjoy. You could do one or a number of the following:

- Plan a trip to a national contest.
- Plan a trip to the Arnold Schwarzenegger Classic.
- Plan a trip to the Mr. Olympia contest.
- Research and find the highest-quality supplements for the best price.
- Order a bodybuilding book from the Home Gym Warehouse to increase your level of knowledge.
- Read a book on motivation.
- Choose a role model to help you in your bodybuilding efforts.
- Learn everything you can about your favorite bodybuilder.
- Learn more about the history and legends of bodybuilding.
- Enter a bodybuilding contest.
- Volunteer to help run a local bodybuilding contest.
- Set the goal of getting your picture in a bodybuilding magazine.

YOU MAY BE GETTING MORE THAN JUST A BETTER BODY

You can grow more from bodybuilding in more ways than merely building big muscles. The courage, discipline, passion, and confidence the lifestyle creates are much more significant to your total quality of life. Maybe those attributes make you a better student or employee. Maybe they make you a better father, mother, son, or daughter. Bodybuilding could enrich your life for many more years to come—so stick with it and work through those illusionary plateaus!

And remember, you won't start getting big until you start thinking big!

Chapter 10

TRAINING SHOULDERS WITH THE INTENSITY FACTOR

BY JASON E. COHEN

If you're like me, you've probably experienced shoulder pain at one time or another. In fact, my shoulders and rotator cuffs are always sore. The trick is to learn to train around shoulder injuries.

Believe it or not, you can get a pretty darn intensive delt workout even if you have nagging shoulder pain. Simply by making a few minor changes in your routine, you can develop massive shoulders.

I advocate movements that emphasize the upper chest. I bring that up because upper-chest training puts a ton of work on the front delts. For example, when you perform the incline press, probably one-third of the movement is direct shoulder work. Most of the pressing exercises you do for chest, especially upper chest, hit your front delts as well. Many shoulder injuries are caused by trainees over-stressing their rotator cuffs. Depending on when you train your shoulders and the bodyparts you work on the same day, you may want to back off on direct front-delt exercises.

START OUT HEAVY

Here's a point with which many trainers and bodybuilders may disagree: You don't have to go superheavy to build big shoulders. The rotator cuff isn't engineered to withstand huge poundages in awkward positions.

Now, there's nothing wrong with using heavy weight on shoulder presses. My point, however, is that, compared to legs, the shoulder is a small muscle group. A good rule of thumb is to start with an exercise you like to go heavy on; say, seated dumbbell presses. The seated dumbbell press is a safer exercise than the barbell variation because your shoulder isn't in as vulnerable a position when you use a barbell. It's also a great exercise to start with because you can go heavy while your shoulders are still fresh. With the dumbbell press you can work around any shoulder pain by repositioning the arc of the press.

I suggest 1 warm-up set of seated dumbbell presses and 3 work sets. If you like to go

Seated dumbbell press—start.

Seated dumbbell press—finish.

heavy, this is your chance. For your work sets choose a weight that allows you to get 5 to 7 reps. This is the only exercise you use heavy weight on, so you want to push the intensity.

KILLER TRI-SET

If you can't tolerate excruciating pain, you should stop reading now. If you're like me and you look forward to pain that will turn your stomach, this is for you. The set is made up of three separate exercises done back-to-back with the same pair of dumbbells: standing dumbbell presses followed by standing front raises followed by dumbbell upright rows. Start with a weight that allows you to do 15 reps on the standing presses. When you finish the set, go immediately into a set of front raises with the same dumbbells for 15 reps. Then, without resting, finish with 15 reps on the upright rows.

If your shoulders don't start burning, you probably aren't using enough weight. If you can barely get 5 reps on the upright rows, you're using too much. This is a great all-around shaping exercise for your shoulders.

The point of the tri-set is to turn up the intensity a level or two. It takes guts to perform a giant set like this one, but the resulting shoulder growth is well worth it. Do two tri-sets and watch your delts grow.

PARTNER-ASSISTED NEGATIVE LATERAL RAISES

As the name suggests, you'll need a partner for this exercise. The funny thing is that you only need a pair of 10-pound dumbbells. It's fun to watch the big guys laugh when I tell them they only need 10-pounders because I know they won't be laughing when the set is over.

Grab the dumbbells and sit on the end of a flat bench in front of a mirror. Have your partner sit directly behind you facing the same direction. Hold the dumbbells out to your sides and have your partner firmly push your arms down. Resist your partner's pressure as much as you can, but don't resist so much that your arms stop or lock out. When your arms are down against your sides, immediately raise them back to the starting position without your partner's resistance. Repeat for 8 reps,

Partner-assisted negative lateral raises.

concentrating on the negative, or downward, portion of the movement. After 8 reps with your partner's resistance, do another 10 reps on your own. Believe me, 10 pounds have never felt so heavy. Do 2 complete sets and get ready to be too weak to hold your water bottle on your own.

REAR-DELT DROP SETS

Many bodybuilders neglect their rear delts because they can't see them, but it doesn't take much to get a killer burn there. I like doing drop sets with relatively light weights to sculpt the area.

When it comes to rear delts, you don't have a lot of exercises to choose from. This program calls for two different movements. For the first exercise you need a stationary incline bench. Turn it in the opposite direction from the way you'd use it for incline presses. Put your chest up against the top of the bench

so you're looking straight into the mirror. Grab a pair of 15-pound dumbbells and do reverse flyes. Once your rear delts are burned out, pick up a pair of 10-pound dumbbells and rep till failure, then switch to a pair of 5-pounders and keep going. You should feel a great burn in the rear delts.

The second rear-delt exercise is drop sets of bent-over reverse cable crossovers. That sounds like a mouthful, but it's actually a very simple movement. Use a weight you can handle for about 8 to 10 reps on your first set. Stand in the middle of the cable rack. Grab the lower-left cable handle with your right hand and the lower-right handle with your left. Bend over to form a 90-degree angle and raise the handles toward the ceiling as if you were doing bent-over laterals. Once you've burned out your rear delts, immediately drop the weight by 20 pounds and get out as many reps as you can. Then lower the weight one more time and give your rear delts the benefit of that final drop.

SIT BACK AND WATCH 'EM GROW

These are only a few sample exercises for blowing out your delts. As long as you don't feel any unnecessary pain in your rotator cuffs when doing your favorite shoulder exercises, you can integrate them into the routine. Remember, your shoulders are small muscles, so don't overdo it. Use heavy weight for your presses and light weight when you raise the iron away from your body.

The timing of your delt workout is also important. As I stated above, you do a lot of front-delt work on chest day. Therefore, you may want to work shoulders and chest on the same day. If you don't, make sure you give your shoulders at least three or four days' rest after your chest workout.

Also, I'm not a big fan of machines when it comes to shoulder training. My experience has been that the machines sort of lock you into one position. Everyone has a different

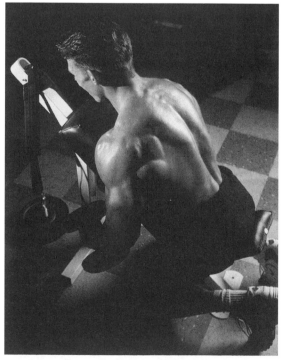

Jonathan Lawson.

pathway of movement on shoulder exercises. Machines, even the best ones, seldom take that into consideration, which is another reason that I like dumbbell movements for quality shoulder growth. Finally, if you're experiencing persistent rotator cuff pain, take a week or two off from direct shoulder work. I guarantee that the amount of stress you put on your shoulders while working your upper chest will cover you until the pain has subsided.

Intensity Shoulder Shocker

Seated dumbbell presses	1 × 10 (warm-up); 3 × 5–7

Tri-set*

Standing dumbbell presses	2 × 15
Front raises	2 × 15
Dumbbell upright rows	2 × 15
Partner-assisted lateral raises**	2 × 18
Incline-bench reverse flyes	1 × triple-drop to failure
Bent-over reverse cable crossovers***	1 × triple-drop to failure

*Use the same pair of dumbbells for all three exercises.

**Perform 8 reps with partner assistance, followed by 10 reps without it.

***Start with 15-pound dumbbells; do 8 reps before the first drop.

Jason Cohen.

Chapter 11

DYNAMITE DELTS

BY DAVE TUTTLE

Great shoulder development is an important part of the exceptional physique all body-builders aspire to. While many bodyparts are larger, few muscles have as much potential for catapulting you to a dominant position on stage. The deltoid forms the top part of the taper you show off with a lat spread. Large lats and a tiny waist certainly help in producing that V-shaped taper, but well-rounded and massive delts can expand its width to eye-popping proportions. The shoulders are also prominently displayed during side-chest shots.

Delt development is more complex than it seems at first glance, however. For example, athletes may do behind-the-neck presses to train the rear portion of their delts. Because of the rotation of the shoulder it's actually the front section that's worked in this movement. Bodybuilders may also fail to recognize the extent to which the front part of the delt is recruited during many chest exercises. If you don't take this into account when designing your shoulder workout, you can overtrain this relatively small muscle. Only a scientifically

developed, balanced training program will provide your shoulders with the right type and amount of stimulus to give you the dynamic delts you seek.

THE FUNCTION OF THE DELTOID MUSCLE

Bodybuilders frequently refer to front delts, side delts, and rear delts, as if there were three deltoid muscles. Anatomically speaking, this is incorrect. There is but one deltoid muscle. It is, however, capable of a variety of different movements, depending on which fibers are recruited. For example, arm flexion, which occurs when you move your arm toward the front of your body, involves the anterior fibers of the deltoid. Arm extension, or moving your arm away from your body toward your back, primarily works the posterior part of the delt. Abduction of the arm, lifting the arm to the side, recruits most of the deltoid's fibers. This distinction is not merely academic. Since the

Ron Coleman.

deltoid is one muscle, it's involved to some extent in every shoulder exercise. You can't isolate your "side delt" and exclude the remainder of the muscle. Failure to understand this has led many bodybuilders to overtrain their shoulders.

The deltoid is a thick, triangular-shaped muscle. It has three points of origin: the clavicle, the scapula, and the acromion process, an extension of the scapula sometimes known as the "shoulder bone." The muscle is inserted on the outside of the humerus, or upper-arm bone.

The deltoid moves with the bones of this region as they are rotated, but it's stronger in some positions than in others. It's important to remember that the portion of the muscle that faces up during an exercise will be recruited the most. Therefore, behind-the-neck presses actually work the front part of the delts, since that's the portion facing upward. Unfortunately, behind-the-neck presses also place a great deal of stress on the tendons and ligaments in the shoulder area. Since there are better exercises for "front delts," you should never do behind-the-neck exercises.

NOVICE WORKOUT

If you're just starting out, you should begin your shoulder training with this exercise:

Standing side raises   3 × 8–12

Always start with a warm-up on each exercise using 40 percent of the weight you will lift on your 3 main sets. This is important because each exercise works the delts somewhat differently. Try to do at least 8 reps per set, and focus on progressive resistance. When you can do 12 reps with a given weight, add more weight. This will temporarily lower the number of reps you can do, but over time you'll gain strength and get up to 12 again. Keep repeating this process, and watch your shoulders go on a growth binge.

Standing side raises will really stimulate growth if you do them correctly. Select a pair of relatively light dumbbells. Stand in front of a mirror so you can watch your form. Begin with your arms at your sides or in front of your upper thighs, with your palms facing inward. Then raise the dumbbells until they're just above your shoulders. Make sure that both arms work in unison, rising at the same time

Paul Jean-Guillaume.

and in the same motion. Stop briefly at the top of the movement, then return the dumbbells to the starting position. Do as many side raises as possible while maintaining good form.

You don't need to raise the dumbbells until they touch, since going the extra distance involves the traps more than the shoulders. Also, make sure that your legs and trunk remain stationary at all times. The goal of this exercise is to isolate the deltoids. Swinging your body back and forth will create momentum and make it easier to lift the dumbbell, as will "shrugging" your traps. Unfortunately, it also makes the exercise less effective. There's no shortcut to superior muscle size, so make sure your technique is perfect even if it means using lighter dumbbells for a while until your delts gain strength.

INTERMEDIATE WORKOUT

The intermediate workout adds another exercise for increased intensity:

Standing side raises	3–4 × 8–12
Rear raises on bench	3–4 × 8–12

If at all possible, use a bench that lets you fully extend your arms when you're lying on it. If the bench has adjustable settings, make it as high as possible off the ground. If your gym only has low benches, you may need to use an angled bench. Or you can sit backward on the type of padded seat often used for incline dumbbell presses. If you use the padded seat, adjust the height of the back of the seat so it's as close to parallel to the ground as possible while still allowing you to fully extend your arms. Although performing this movement at an angle is not as effective at isolating the rear fibers of your delts as using a flat bench, it still recruits them for most of the work.

Select a pair of relatively light dumbbells and place them on both sides of the bench. Lie on the bench so that your head is floating in the air but your entire trunk is supported. Grab the dumbbells with your palms facing each other. Keeping your elbows nearly locked-out at all times, lift both dumbbells simultaneously until your arms are parallel to the floor. Be careful not to move your torso; this is not a back exercise. Hold the dumbbells in the parallel position for a second or so, then slowly lower them to the starting position in a controlled movement. Repeat for the designated number of repetitions.

ADVANCED WORKOUT

The advanced workout includes the two exercises of the intermediate workout plus an additional exercise for the front part of the delts:

Standing side raises	4 × 8–12
Rear raises on bench	4 × 8–12
Seated dumbbell presses	4 × 8–12

Perform the seated dumbbell presses in front of a mirror to help you maintain perfect form. Since the dumbbells are lifted closer to your trunk during this movement than they are during the other two exercises, you'll be able to use dumbbells that are at least twice as

Bertil Fox.

heavy as the ones you use for the other movements. Select a pair of relatively heavy dumbbells and place them in front of a padded seat. Adjust the back of the seat so it's as vertical as possible.

Pick up the dumbbells with your palms facing each other. In a single movement, clean the dumbbells to just above your shoulders and sit down. The dumbbells should be

6 inches from the top of your shoulders, and your palms should be facing forward. Press the dumbbells up until your arms are straight and your hands are slightly wider than shoulder width. Make sure both arms move together and always keep your trunk stationary. Don't "shrug" your traps to help lift the weight, and never curve your spine. Your back should remain against the seat at all times. Now lower the weights to the starting position next to your shoulders and repeat.

HEAD AND SHOULDERS ABOVE THE REST

If you use these techniques and exercises, you'll be well on your way to building shoulders that will set you apart from the average bodybuilder. Remember to use the principle of progressive resistance, and listen to the signals your body sends you about the need for recuperation. You'll soon develop the dynamic delts of your dreams.

Chapter 12

NATURAL CHEST TRAINING

BY JASON E. COHEN

How do you know when your training intensity is high enough? When I'm asked that question, I usually answer with a question: Could you have gotten 2 more reps with that weight before you racked it? If your answer is yes, you're not training intensely enough. So how do you increase your intensity? You have to change your mind-set when you're in the gym. Your mind is a lot more powerful than your muscles will ever be. Before you do a set, you have to tell yourself that you're going to get 2 more reps than you got last week—and do it. In order to take your body to a new level, you must increase your threshold for pain.

A GRUELING CHEST MATCH

There are plenty of exercises and variations of exercises for the chest. Nevertheless, after training hundreds of bodybuilders, I've observed that most trainees lack upper-chest development. I'm talking about the kind of

chest you could lean your own chin on—the kind that Arnold bragged he could set a glass of water on. Not only does a strong upper chest look impressive, but it tends to highlight your middle-chest development as well. I'd also go so far as to say that the weight of a massive upper chest will push your pecs down so that you achieve the look of a hanging lower chest.

VARIATION IS THE KEY

The trick to keeping your muscles from adapting to any one routine is very simple: Change your routine frequently. There are so many good exercises that hit the pecs directly that it shouldn't be difficult. It's important to pick movements that isolate and put as much stress on the chest as possible. For that reason alone the bench press isn't your best option because the assisting muscles, the triceps and shoulders, get too much attention. Obviously, there's no way to isolate any muscle group

Dumbbell bench press—start.   Mike O'Hearn.

Dumbbell bench press—finish.

completely without using some assisting muscles. Here are some variations and techniques that are guaranteed to turn up the intensity.

Warm up for intensity

Due to the difficulty of the exercises it's a good idea to warm up your chest fully before you jump into them. I like to warm up by preexhausting my chest with some moderately heavy cable crossovers. The cable crossover is also a great stretching exercise to get your chest ready for a grueling session. I suggest 3 sets of 6 to 8 reps: On the first set, cross the handles directly in front of your chest and hold them in that position for about four seconds; on the next set hold them crossed in front of your neck for four seconds, and on the final set hold them crossed at hip level for four seconds. That should get your blood flowing and get you adequately warmed up.

Incline dumbbell press—start.

A superintense superset

For the two exercises you'll need a standard bench press setup and a pair of dumbbells. The weights you use depend on your strength level. Set the bar on the bench press with an amount you can comfortably handle for 30 reps. Most trainees—even some of the strongest guys I've trained—use one 45-pound plate on each side. As for the dumbbells, they should be slightly lighter than you normally use for regular dumbbell bench presses.

This combination involves doing a set of flat-bench dumbbell presses followed by a burnout set of barbell presses, but you perform the dumbbell presses with a slight variation. Lie on the bench as you would for a set of flat-bench dumbbell presses but slide all the way down the bench until only your shoulder blades and head are still supported. Your butt should be practically touching the ground, and your body should be balanced on your feet and shoulder blades.

Perform a set of 8 to 12 dumbbell presses in this position, and when you're done, immediately put down the dumbbells, slide up the

Incline dumbbell press—finish.

bench, pick up the barbell, and do as many presses as you can. You'll be burning big time in no time. Do 3 supersets in this manner. Increase the weight if you need to up the intensity.

Drop sets to raise the pain threshold

This one uses the incline dumbbell press. Keeping in mind the need for variety, I've included two different drop-set routines for you to try:

Drop Set 1   Set an incline bench at a 45-degree angle and get 3 sets of dumbbells that are 10 pounds apart, with the heaviest being a weight you can handle for 6 reps. On your first set, go to failure with the heaviest weights, then immediately grab the dumbbells that are 10 pounds lighter and do a set to failure. After that—you guessed it—you immediately grab the third set of dumbbells and rep

to failure. If your muscles aren't burning after that, something is wrong.

Drop Set 2   Technically, this is an up-the-rack sequence, not a drop, because you go up in weight on each set but decrease the angle. Adjust the incline so that it's two notches higher than 45 degrees and again select 3 sets of dumbbells that are 10 pounds apart. Perform your first set for 10 reps with the lightest weights, then immediately set the incline down one notch and grab the next heaviest set of dumbbells. Do 10 reps or go to failure, then drop the dumbbells, drop the incline to 45 degrees, and perform a set with the heaviest weights you choose for 10 reps or to failure.

The exercises are very grueling, and you probably won't be able to do the supersets and the incline triple drops on the same day. There's a fine line between high intensity and overtraining. You must learn your limitations so you don't cross it.

(2)

Incline dumbbell press with triple drops (1).

(3)

CREATE YOUR OWN CHEST-CRUSHING ROUTINE

Onc simplc solution to the need for variety is to change your order of exercises frequently. Another is to do one of the two intense workouts just described with one or two of your favorite exercises and then switch at the next chest workout.

Pay attention to the areas of your chest that need the most work. If you have a weak upper chest, start with and emphasize incline movements. If you have a weak inner chest, try incline cable crossovers and standing cable crossovers. Just train intelligently. As stated previously, your mind is much more powerful than any muscle in your body.

Chest Blaster 1
Cable crossovers*   3 × 6–8

*Include a four-second pause in the fully contracted position and do one set with the hands crossed in front of the chest, one with the hands crossed in front of the neck, and one with the hands crossed in front of thc hips.

Jason Cohen.

Cable crossovers.   Mike O'Hearn.

Superset
Dumbbell bench presses* 3 × 8–12
Barbell bench presses   3 × failurc

*Performed at foot of bench with body supported by shoulders and feet.

Chest Blaster 2
Cable crossovers*   3 × 6–8

*Include a four-second pause in the fully contracted position and do 1 set with the hands crossed in front of the chest, 1 with the hands crossed in front of the neck, and 1 with the hands crossed in front of the hips.

45-degree incline
    dumbbell presses*   3 × failure

*Perform as 1 triple-drop set, going down the rack without stopping, and use dumbbells that are 10 pounds lighter on each successive round.

OR
Incline-dumbbell
    presses*   3 × 10 or failure

*Perform as 1 giant set, going up the rack without stopping, and use dumbbells that are 10 pounds heavier while dropping the angle on each successive round.

Chapter 13

BASEBALL BICEPS

BY DAVE TUTTLE

There's no question that biceps development is high on most bodybuilders' priority list. That may seem strange, since the biceps is clearly one of the smaller muscle groups. Even with the most gargantuan development, its size pales in comparison with the quadriceps or back. Yet whatever logic may dictate, bodybuilders are emotionally drawn to the king of bodyparts: the biceps.

Trainees have two main goals with this muscle group: achieving maximum circumference and the highest peak. The two don't necessarily go hand in hand. The biceps area could be thick and relatively flat, or it could be thin yet soar upward in a towering peak.

THE FUNCTION OF THE BICEPS MUSCLES

The area commonly known as the biceps is technically referred to as the anterior humeral region, and it includes the coraco-brachialis, the biceps brachii, and the brachialis anticus. The coraco-brachialis is the smallest of the three. It's located in the upper and inner part of the arm. It originates at a bony area near the collarbone known as the coracoid process and inserts onto the middle of the humerus, or upper-arm bone, by means of a flat tendon. The coraco-brachialis permits adduction of the arm, which is the action of bringing it toward the trunk. It also helps elevate the arm toward the scapula, the shoulder blade.

The biceps brachii is by far the largest muscle in the region. It has two origins, which is why we say *biceps* instead of *bicep*. The short head originates at the coracoid process, where it is fused with the coraco-brachialis, while the long head originates from the upper portion of the glenoid cavity, an oval-shaped depression that the head of the humerus bone fits into. The two heads join about halfway down the humerus. The biceps inserts below the elbow on the radius, which is the smaller of the forearm bones.

Flex Wheeler.

This muscle flexes the elbow and supinates, or rotates, the radius. You can observe this supination by placing your forearm at a 90-degree angle to the upper arm and turning your hand from palm-down to palm-up.

The brachialis anticus is a broad muscle that covers the elbow joint and the lower half of the front of the humerus. It originates on the humerus and inserts on the front surface of the ulna, which is the larger forearm bone. It is a major flexor of the elbow and protects the elbow joint as well.

THREE-LEVEL PROGRAM

Always start with a warm-up on every exercise using 40 percent of the weight you'll lift on your 3 main sets. This is important because each exercise works the muscles differently. Try to do at least 6 reps per set, and focus on progressive resistance. When you can do 10 reps with a given weight, increase the weight.

This will temporarily lower the number of reps you can do, but over time you'll gain strength and work up to 10 reps again. Keep repeating this process, and watch as your biceps muscles balloon in size and shape.

Novice workout

Since these three muscles are recruited to some extent every time you train chest, back, or shoulders, it's very easy to overtrain the biceps. In fact, overtraining may be as much a factor in holding back your growth as improper exercise technique. To ensure that you don't overtrain, the novice workout includes only one exercise. This will allow you to use maximum intensity in executing the movement.

Dumbbell curls 3×6–10

You can perform dumbbell curls either seated on a bench or standing up. In both cases, however, only your arms should move. You must keep the rest of your body stationary. The goal here is to isolate the biceps muscles. If you swing your body, you defeat the purpose.

Take a dumbbell in each hand and hold them at your sides with your palms facing your legs. Now rotate one of your palms so that it faces forward and begin the movement. Bring the weight up until the biceps is completely contracted and the dumbbell is almost touching your shoulder. Keep your upper arm next to your side. Twist the dumbbell at the top so that your little finger is forced closest to the shoulder. This provides the fullest contraction. Lower the arm to the starting position and do the same movement with your other arm. Continue alternating arms until you complete the required reps.

If you find that you're stronger in one arm than the other, start with the weaker arm. Continue to alternate your arms as indicated above, forcing out repetitions until you can't get any more with the weaker arm, then stop—even if you could do more with your stronger arm. In time this should reduce the strength differential.

Intermediate workout

The intermediate workout includes a second exercise for added development.

Dumbbell curls	3–4×6–10
Preacher curls	3–4×6–10

If you use it properly, the preacher bench eliminates all cheating from the curling movement. Therefore, you probably won't be able to lift as much weight as you can on biceps exercises that permit swinging.

Select a relatively light dumbbell. (If you're not sure how much you can lift, err on the side of caution for your first set.) Place your arm firmly on the portion of the preacher bench that's at a 45-degree angle to the floor. Put a dumbbell in the hand of your weaker arm. Position your upper arm so that the biceps brachii and your palm are facing directly upward.

Without moving your trunk or shoulders, slowly lift the dumbbell until your forearm touches your biceps. Crunch your forearm against the biceps and pull the dumbbell as close to your shoulder as you can without bending your wrist. This will give your biceps brachii and brachialis anticus a great workout. (Since the arm is stationary on the preacher bench, the coraco-brachialis isn't called into play.) Slowly lower the weight to its original position and repeat.

Once you've performed as many repetitions as you can with your weaker arm, repeat the exercise with your stronger arm. Stop after you do the same number of repetitions you did with your weaker arm.

Advanced workout

The elite routine piles on the intensity with a third exercise.

Dumbbell curls	4×6–10
Preacher curls	4×6–10
Standing ez-curl bar curls	4×6–10

An ez-curl bar is a cambered barbell that has a Z shape. Place the ez-curl bar in front of you. Position your feet at approximately

shoulder width. Let your arms hang naturally at your sides, then rotate them slightly so that your thumbs point directly ahead. This will put your palms at an approximate 45-degree angle to your legs.

Squat and place your hands on the two parts of the bar that most closely match the positioning of your hands. Grip the bar and stand up. Without swinging your body or moving your shoulders, lift the bar until your forearms are as close to your biceps as possible. Your upper arms should remain close to your sides. Crunch your biceps. Then lower the bar to the starting position and repeat.

Sometimes bodybuilders try to raise the cambered bar even farther so that their upper arms are parallel to the ground at the end of the movement. The last part of the motion

recruits the shoulders but not the biceps. Once your forearm is next to your upper arm, the biceps has contracted as much as it can. Train your shoulders on shoulder day.

BICEPS PEAKS AND GENETICS

There's a great deal of misunderstanding about the role of genetics in the development of a great biceps peak. Sometimes athletes are told that they can train the "middle" of the biceps brachii to increase its peak. Alas, there's no truth to this rumor. The physical relationship between your biceps brachii's length and its height is determined genetically and cannot be altered. No exercise will enable you to get a greater peak per se, but the greater the volume of all three of your biceps muscles, the higher your peak will be when you contract them.

The best course of action is to train your biceps muscles properly with full intensity and sufficient recuperation. Avoid overtraining and allow your guns to grow to their full genetic potential. Here's another tip: When you flex your arms during competition, make sure that you leave a space between your biceps and forearm. When the judges see your biceps peak next to the depth of your elbow joint, it will seem even higher. It may be an optical illusion, but who cares?

So blast your guns into massive proportions and show them off correctly. Those baseball-sized biceps you've dreamed about can be yours!

Chapter 14

NATURAL BACK ATTACK

BY JASON E. COHEN

I've seen more bodybuilding contests than I care to remember, and I've also competed in more bodybuilding contests than I care to remember. The one thing that stands out in my mind is how many of those shows were won or lost solely on the impressiveness of the athletes' back development.

Yet the back tends to be overlooked in the gym. For some reason you always hear people say things like, "Jeez, look at the size of those arms!" or, "Check out the wheels on that guy!" You rarely, however, hear people say, "That is one thick back!" Since you can't see your own back, it's easy to drop the intensity on your back training. In addition, the back is a difficult muscle group to train due to the intricacy of its architecture. Consider how many muscles it includes: the latissimus dorsi, rhomboideus, infraspinatus, teres major, teres minor, and trapezius.

What's the most effective way to build an impressive back? I like to approach my back workouts with a specific plan of attack. The

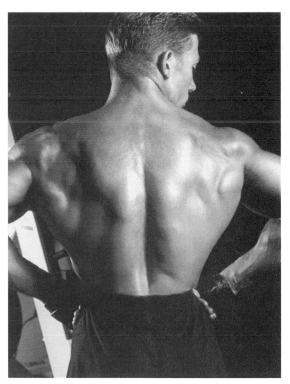

Jonathan Lawson.

trick is to accomplish my goals without overtraining.

For the time being forget about the poundages you currently use on your back exercises. Instead, lighten the weight and concentrate on squeezing, holding, and contracting your back muscles on each and every set. That's something you rarely see in the gym. It's also the primary reason that so many people fail to get really sore back muscles the day after a back workout.

You also want to concentrate on your form. On pulling and rowing exercises stick your chest out, slightly arch your back, keep your elbows in tight, and squeeze your shoulder blades together. That sounds like a lot to do, but it's critical. I can't emphasize enough the importance of feeling your back work while you train it.

If you follow those simple tips, you'll be forced to drop the weight from what you're used to lifting. I guarantee that the detail and thickness you'll develop in your back will be worth it.

Keep in mind that you don't do all of the exercises I suggest at every workout. You only do one exercise for each of the three criteria—width, thickness, and power and strength—and an additional exercise for the area in which you think you may be weakest. Otherwise, you could fall into the overtraining trap.

Pulldowns.   Karl List.

EXERCISES FOR WIDTH

If you want to add some serious width to your back, I suggest a couple of different exercises. I like to start my back training with wide-grip chinups to the front. Chins are usually a good warm-up exercise because you only work with your bodyweight. If you're more advanced and really want to blast it, add some weight to a belt.

I often see people performing this exercise incorrectly. Maybe that's because it's misnamed. Technically speaking, they aren't chins, they're "chests." When you pull your body up toward the bar, your upper chest—

not your chin—should literally touch the bar. Concentrate on your back and control your tempo. Try to take the biceps out of the movement. You may want to use straps so that you can really isolate your back. Start with 3 sets, going to complete failure on each set.

Another good exercise for adding back width is wide-grip pulldowns to the front. I don't recommend doing them to the back because it puts your shoulder girdle in a compromising position. If you do have shoulder problems—as 85 percent of bodybuilders do—you may want to try close-grip pulldowns instead. I've found that close-grips don't put quite as much pressure on the rotator cuff. Whichever you decide to do, I recommend 3 sets to failure, going up in weight on each successive set.

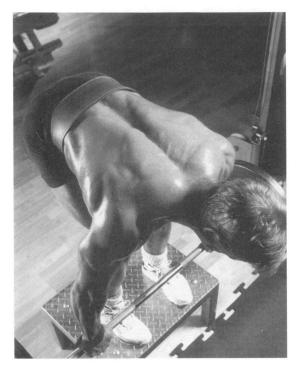

Barbell row—start.

Barbell row—finish.

T-bar rows.　　　　　　　　Michael Ashley.

EXERCISES FOR THICKNESS

I've found that using a variety of rowing exercises builds back thickness. The list of effective movements includes close-grip seated rows, bent-over rows, T-bar rows, and cable rows.

Once again, form is key. Keep these three basic points in mind:

1. Lean back slightly and pull to your chest.
2. Arch your back.
3. Squeeze your shoulder blades together.

Another great exercise to try is seated close-grip pulldowns to the front. You'll need a double-handled V-bar and a pulldown machine. I also strongly suggest that you use a spotter. To ensure that I am fully contracting my back muscles, I add a little twist to this exercise. Decrease the weight you use on the movement by about 40 pounds. Position yourself firmly on the apparatus with your legs under the support pad and your arms directly above your head. Have your partner or spotter stick his or her finger between your shoulder

Low-pulley row.

blades, and on each rep squeeze your spotter's finger. That guarantees a full contraction and that you're really squeezing your back on each rep. As you'll discover, it doesn't take much weight to get an intense burn. Try doing 3 sets with this technique and get ready to feel some pain the next day.

Since my weakness seems to be thickness, I do two exercises for that area. For my second exercise I usually pick a different rowing movement each time. I also like to do cross-bench dumbbell pullovers every once in a while. Variety is a great way to get your back sore each and every time you train it. I'm convinced that muscle has memory—if you can throw something new in, it will keep your muscles guessing.

EXERCISES FOR POWER AND STRENGTH

Up to this point you were probably thinking that you wanted to give this program a try. Well, it just wouldn't be any fun without a grueling exercise like—you guessed it—dead-

lifts. The reason people hate deadlifts is that they suck. They're tough and intense, and they require a lot of concentration. But, generally speaking, the more grueling an exercise is, the more effective it is.

Deadlifts are so difficult because they involve many different bodyparts and require quite a bit of technique. If you don't deadlift regularly, start slowly and concentrate on your form. I prefer deadlifting off the floor with a 45-pound plate beneath my feet. Here are some points to remember when deadlifting:

1. Keep your body tight.
2. Keep your head slightly tilted toward the ceiling.
3. Start and finish the movement with the bar touching your shins.

Since so many different muscles are involved, I like to be warmed up, so I usually do deadlifts as my second exercise.

When it comes to sets and reps for the deadlift, there are many schools of thought. It helps to remember that your goal is bodybuilding, not powerlifting. You don't need to

Deadlift—start.

Deadlift—finish.   Will Willis.

use huge amounts of weight to build a quality back. I like to mix it up a little. Usually I do 1 warm-up set and 4 work sets of deadlifts. Some days I concentrate on high reps in the 12 to 15 range and on others I increase the poundages and do low reps in the 3 to 5 range. Then on other days I do a warm-up, 3 low-rep sets, and finish with 1 high-rep set. Don't be afraid to vary your deadlifting and make it more fun—although *fun* may not be the correct word. Also, you can vary your foot and hand positions to change your deadlifting technique.

One final note on deadlifting. It's very important to concentrate on involving your whole back. Try to avoid pulling with your hamstrings, traps, biceps, and lower back. Once you get the technique down, you'll see vast improvements in your back development in no time.

BACK TO THE BASICS

By now I hope you're thinking that it's easier than you imagined to build an impressive back. It is, assuming you get a really good mind/muscle connection on your sets. Concentrate on the way you want your back to look as you squeeze and contract on every rep. So with all of the above in mind go out and attack your back!

One-arm dumbbell row.   Jason Cohen.

Yohnnie Shambourger.

Chapter 15

EXTRAORDINARY BACK TRAINING

BY YOHNNIE SHAMBOURGER

It's not unusual to have huge arms. It's not unusual to have sweeping quads or a Herculean chest. If you want to dominate on the bodybuilding stage year after year, you must have an extraordinary back. Just ask Lee Haney. Just ask Dorian Yates. The common denominator is always the same.

The back is the centerpiece of your physique. It defines your symmetry, and an effective lat spread can make you look as if you have wings. Even so, many athletes rob themselves of complete back development when they train. Since you can't see your back when you work it, it's easy to make mistakes—mistakes that can hamper your growth and stall your advancement in the sport.

Back training requires a pulling action. The first major problem occurs when you put too much biceps power into the movement. That's a concern for beginning bodybuilders as well as for many experienced professionals. It's a natural reflex to pull with your arms first and them employ the back as a secondary muscle group. This is wrong! You're training

Yohnnie Shambourger.

Wide-grip pullups.

your back, so think back. Initiate the pulling action from your back. As you continue pulling the weight, shift the stress past your biceps and onto your shoulder blades and latissimus dorsi, muscles that are much larger and more powerful than your biceps can ever be.

The next major problem occurs when you attempt to pull heavy weight without using wrist straps. Too often your grip gives out before your back does. Wrist straps allow you to relax your grip and concentrate on the section of your back you're targeting. Without the straps you'll find yourself tiring and gradually shifting the emphasis from your back to your arms. So, when the judges ask for a back double-biceps pose, all they'll notice is the size of your arms and the lack of size and definition in your back. If you avoid wrist straps because you can never get them to feel secure, you're probably using an over-the-bar instead of an under-the-bar wrap. Wrap your straps along the length of the bar so your hands can rest evenly over it. Never train your back without wrist straps!

In designing your back-training program, remember that the major muscles in the back are the trapezius, posterior deltoid, teres major, rhomboid, latissimus dorsi, and erector spinae. To effectively stimulate those muscle groups, you should divide your back into three focal points, the upper, middle, and lower back. That makes it easier to concentrate on your total back without neglecting areas you cannot see. When working any of the focal points, you should feel stress only in that target area. If you don't, you should immediately recognize that something isn't right and make adjustments. They could be as simple as changing the height of your seat, readjusting your hand position, or just relaxing your arms and slowing your movements. Which exercises are most effective for back training? There are many choices, but the most common exercises are the following.

Upper Back
Upright rows
Pulldowns
Wide-grip pullups
High-grip T-bar rows
Shrugs

Bent-over rows—start.

Bent-over rows—finish.

Middle Back
Bent-over rows
Machine seated rows
One-arm dumbbell rows
Low-grip T-bar rows

Lower Back
Deadlifts
Seated cable rows
Hyperextensions

When performing the exercises, keep in mind the following points.

Upright rows

Always keep your elbows higher than your hands. Don't rush this movement. Slow, deliberate reps are best. Never allow your upper body to jerk backward, placing your lower back into excessive extension, or hyperlordosis. Use light to moderate weight.

Pulldowns

It's natural to start this exercise with your arms—don't do it. Initiate the movement in your back by pulling your shoulder blades downward. Relax the stress in your hands and arms so you can concentrate on the back. Use moderate weight.

Wide-grip pullups

This exercise can be very demanding on your body during the off-season if you're very heavy, so be careful. You can easily strain your shoulders. Always warm up before performing this exercise. Use your bodyweight only—*don't add weight.*

High-grip T-bar rows

Keep your back straight, and try to keep your body nearly parallel to the floor. Avoid raising

Lat pulldown—start.

Lat pulldown—finish.

Upright row—start.

Upright row—finish.

One-arm dumbbell row—start.

your torso during this exercise. That usually occurs when the weight is too heavy and you overcompensate. Instead, draw your elbows upward, pinching your shoulder blades together. Use moderate weight.

Shrugs

Never lower your head to your shoulders. This causes unnecessary stress on your neck. Keep your head up and bring your shoulders to your ears. Don't roll your shoulders. Use heavy weight.

Bent-over rows

This is a great exercise and most effective when you perform it at the start of your back routine. Keep your back straight and pull the bar into your waist, not toward your chest. Use moderate to heavy weight.

Machine seated rows

Keep your chest up and pressed into the pad, and don't overextend your arms.

One-arm dumbbell row—finish.

Overextension on the eccentric, or negative, phase of the rep shifts the stress off your back and turns your back workout into an arm and shoulder workout. Use moderate to heavy weight.

One-arm dumbbell rows

Keep your elbows close to your body. Start with the weight in a fully extended position, then draw the dumbbell up and back toward your hips. Use moderate to heavy weight.

Low-grip T-bar rows

Keep your elbows close to your sides. Avoid overextending your reach on the negative part of the rep. Use heavy weight.

Deadlifts

Be careful: The standard deadlift can cause lower-back pain. Take it slow and don't start off too heavy. Keep your back straight, your head up, and the bar close to or touching your body. Use moderate to heavy weight.

Seated cable rows

Don't rush this one—use a slow and deliberate movement. Draw your elbows back, keeping them close to your body, and keep your chest up. Be careful not to jerk your lower back. Use moderate weight.

Hyperextensions

Keep your hips on the pad. If your hips are too far off the pad, you'll no longer be training your lower back but instead will be working hamstrings. Use light weight.

Now that you have the facts, you can retool your back-training routine. The next time you step on stage, they won't just notice the size of your arms. They'll also notice your extraordinary back.

Chapter 16

NATURAL QUAD TRAINING

BY JASON E. COHEN

A couple of days ago a guy came up to me in the gym and accused my training partner and me of being on the juice. My training partner happens to be the reigning Natural Mr. America, and I've won quite a few natural contests myself. We pride ourselves on training as hard as we possibly can on every rep of every set of every session. Nevertheless, this guy was convinced that we were chemically enhanced. I simply said to him, "Have you ever seen us train?" He looked at me kind of confused and said no. I invited him to work out with us, and he reluctantly said he'd love to. When I told him to pick his favorite bodypart to train, he blurted with a smile, "Legs!" Big mistake.

As usual, John and I started with our favorite exercise, squats. Unlike most bodybuilders, we do a different squat routine at every workout. On that day we happened to be doing one we call D-Day. Our new training partner still had that smile and swagger when he said he liked the name. John and I just looked at each other.

We started with a warm-up set of 135 pounds for 10 quick reps. We told our new training partner we only did 3 sets after our warm-up, and once again he looked at us as if we were sissies. Our next set was actually another warm-up, with 185 pounds for 10 quick reps to get the blood flowing. Then came the big one, a set in which we squat 225 pounds for 51 reps.

Yes, you read that correctly: We stop at 51 reps or when the weight crashes to the floor, whichever comes first.

I stepped up to the bar and got through my first 35 reps with some discomfort, but I was determined to get 16 more. With each rep came more excruciating pain. I got to 48, and the weight dropped to the safety rack. I was exhausted and had tears running down my face.

John was next, and I could tell he was feeling good. He went all out and blasted 52 reps, then fell to the floor. After that our new training partner, with a look of sheer terror, positioned himself under the squat bar. To our

surprise he did pretty well. He got 32 good reps and then racked it.

I said, "Wait a minute. The rule is that you end your set at the safety bars at the bottom, not the top pins." With sweat running down his face, he just snarled at me.

After that we threw 315 pounds on the bar and did a final burnout for 10 reps. Our new training partner squeaked out 4. We were not finished with our leg routine—not by a long shot.

Next up was the leg press. When we told our new partner that we were only doing 1 set, we saw the first smile on his face since the routine began. What he didn't know was, the set would be for 100 reps: 10 sets of 10 without taking our feet off the pressing platform. I went first and was nearly dying when I got to my rep number 70. I knew I had to get 30 or more, or John would be yelling so loud that the whole gym would watch me suffer. I got the 30 and collapsed on the floor until the lactic acid slowly left my quads.

John went next and didn't feel excruciating pain until he got to about rep number 85. After that it was a dogfight, but he won. Our new training partner tentatively sat in the leg press and started his routine. John and I could see he was suffering beyond what we'd seen on the squat rack. He ended up getting 30 reps before the platform crashed to the bottom position. He was done and in agony.

Before we began our third and final exercise, leg extensions, our new training partner went into the locker room. This is where the story gets a little scary. He went to the bathroom and collapsed, hitting his head on the floor. Someone happened to see it and called for help. An ambulance took him to the emergency room. I have seen him at the gym since that day, but, needless to say, he hasn't volunteered to train with us again.

As you can see from the above, John and I don't mess around when we train legs. It's my opinion that a great physique is built from the ground up. This chapter includes routines for

Stiff-legged deadlift—start.

Stiff-legged deadlift—finish.

Leg extension.   James De Melo.

both quads and hamstrings. It's entirely up to you whether you choose to work the two bodyparts on the same day.

Keep in mind that these intensity-loaded programs were designed for experienced weight trainers. I don't recommend that you try to do them on the day after you read this article. Adjust the weights and reps to your level of experience and work your way up. The only requirement is that you give it all you've got on every rep of every set.

ALL-OUT QUAD ASSAULT

Squat Routine 1: D-Day
This routine is guaranteed to shock your legs into growth. Here's the complete workout:

Barbell squats

(warm-up)	2×12
(work sets)	1×50

Use a weight you can handle with perfect form for 50.

$1 \times 8\text{--}10$

Use the heaviest weight you can.

Leg presses   1 × 100

You may pause after every 10 reps, but don't remove your feet from the platform.

Leg extensions   3 × failure

Continue the reps as follows until your legs are burning:

- On set 1 perform one fast extension followed by one with a three-second pause at the top.
- On set 2 do 3 fast reps followed by one three-second pause at the top.
- On set 3 do 3 fast reps followed by one slow rep at the top.

Squat routine 2: 10 Till You Topple

This program is guaranteed to get your legs and your heart in great shape. Some people refer to it as German volume training. As with all of these routines, I recommend that you use a spotter. You'll also need a flat bench and a watch with a second hand.

To complete the routine, do 10 sets of squats for 10 repetitions each. The tough part is that you can't fool around between sets. You perform each set 30 seconds after your partner's sets.

While your partner does his or her set, you should be stretching the fascia in your quads on the flat bench. You do this by putting one foot top down on the bench—that is, on the shoelaces—and sitting on it. Your bent leg should be hanging off the bench with your knee pointing at the floor. Stretch your quad. Your quad should feel as if it's going to explode out of your skin.

Remember, you should be going down to slightly past parallel on every squat repetition. If you can't go down that far on every rep, lighten the weight until your form is perfect. Also, don't guess on the 30 seconds between sets—use a stopwatch.

Finish the workout with leg extensions. Perform 5 sets to failure, taking turns with your partner on the machine, with one jumping on as soon as the other is finished.

The complete 10 Till You Topple routine looks like this:

Squats   10 × 10

Stretch your quads while your partner is training, then rest only 30 seconds between sets.

Leg press—start.

Chris Faildo.

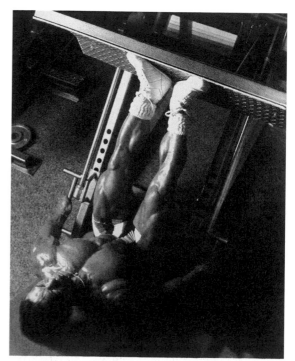

Leg press—finish.

Leg extensions   5 × failure

Rest only long enough for your partner to do his or her set.

Squat Routine 3

This workout, if you do it properly, may be the toughest of the three. It's based on the tempo of the repetitions. Once again, the routine starts with a variation of the squat. You perform 6 sets with a very slow cadence: six seconds down and six seconds up. When doing your reps, have your partner count to six until you reach a point slightly below parallel, then count to six again as you come up. In this case, however, you don't stop at the top. Instead, start the next rep immediately.

Do as many reps in this manner as you can until your partner has to help you rack it or until you dump the weight on the safety rack. Perform 1 warm-up set and then do 5 work sets. Go as slowly as you can. Your legs will be burning to the point where they'll start to shake. Make sure you have a spotter and a safety rack handy when you do these squats.

Squat—start.

Squat—finish.

The next exercise in the routine is walking lunges. For some reason bodybuilders don't like this movement. My guess is that they think it looks goofy and that there's no ego involved. I beg to differ. Try 3 sets back-to-back with your partner. In other words, trade off and don't waste time. Simply take two moderately heavy dumbbells and lunge from one end of the gym to the other and back to the starting point. Your legs will burn, and you'll be sweating so much you'll feel as if you're going to collapse. That's good. It means you're training with intensity.

Here's the complete workout:

Squats	6 × failure
(Slow cadence: six seconds down and six seconds up)	
Walking lunges	× 3
(Two lengths of the gym floor equals 1 set)	

SOME FINAL THOUGHTS ON QUAD TRAINING

The three routines outlined above are extremely demanding. You probably noticed that none of them takes a lot of time to complete. To stay focused and train with the intensity these workouts demand, you must keep your workouts short. In addition, there's nothing wrong with throwing in an extra exercise, depending on your particular weakness in leg development. The key is not to overdo it. If you can perform many more exercises after getting through any of these routines, you didn't train hard enough.

HAMSTRING HELPER

I haven't figured out the reason so many bodybuilders neglect their hamstrings, but I assume it's because they can't see them. The irony is, they can't see them because they don't train them hard enough. As I said above, I leave it to you to determine if you like to work hams and quads on the same day. For me it depends on

how much working my quads takes out of me. Usually I end up training quads and hams on different days.

In the Hamstring Helper routine, you start with lying leg curls. Begin with a weight you can handle for about 12 reps, and use that as your warm-up set. After that you jump into some killer drop sets (descending sets). Make sure your hams are properly warmed up so you don't pull or tear a muscle. Start with a weight that you can get 4 to 5 reps with, then drop the weight by two plates and repeat, continuing the progression all the way up the stack for 5 reps on each weight. On the last drop, do a set of 10. If your maximum for 4 to 5 reps is not very high, then drop the weight by only one plate each time. You should be doing approximately 6 sets on each giant drop set. Perform 3 giant sets, adjusting the weight appropriately for each set.

The next exercise is straight-bar stiff-legged deadlifts performed for 4 sets at a slow tempo. Start with a warm-up set, stretching your hams at the bottom of the movement. After you're properly warmed up, add some weight to the bar. The rep tempo for the second set is three seconds down and six seconds up. Perform as many reps as you can in this manner. You'll feel your hams and lower back burning.

You finish off with seated leg curls. Instead of just performing a curl and then letting the weight swing your legs back to the top of the movement, use the following cadence: Stop halfway down and hold for three seconds, then go to the bottom of the movement and hold for three seconds. Do not let the weight swing to the top. Instead stop halfway up and hold for three seconds. Perform as many reps as you can in this manner until your hams are fried.

Here's the complete workout:

Lying Leg Curls	
(warm-up)	1 × 12
Giant sets	3 × 4–5

Do six drops down the weight stack for each giant set, performing 10 reps on the last drop of each set.

Stiff-legged deadlifts   4 × failure
(Slow cadence: three seconds down and
  six seconds up)

Seated leg curls   3 × failure
(Cadence: Hold for three seconds when
  you get halfway to the bottom of the
  rep, at the bottom, and at the halfway
  point on the way up.)

Unfortunately, there's not as much variety when it comes to leg biceps training, but that doesn't mean you can't make it intense and interesting. For example, instead of lying leg curls, throw the following exercise into the above routine.

Dumbbell leg curls

Grab a flat bench and lie facedown on it with your knees at the end of the bench. Have your partner put a dumbbell you can handle for 10 to 15 reps between your feet, with your feet close together and holding it up at one end. Curl the weight just as you would on a lying curl machine. Instead of quitting after this set, work all the way down the rack. Have your partner drop the weight by 10 pounds until there are no smaller dumbbells on the rack.

SOME FINAL THOUGHTS ON HAMSTRING TRAINING

Just because you can't see them doesn't mean they're not there. If you choose to train your hams on the same day as your quads, you may try alternating the order, working hamstrings first at every other leg session. If you're lagging in hamstring development, however, be sure to put more emphasis on that bodypart.

SIT BACK AND WATCH 'EM GROW

As we all know too well, there are so many factors that contribute to muscle growth. Few factors, however, are as important as training intensity. I'm willing to bet that if you give the above routines a try, you'll experience serious growth. Don't be afraid to experiment with varying the routines to fit your specific needs. The bottom line is, if you train with intensity, your muscles will grow.

Jason Cohen.

Chapter 17

TOTAL INTENSITY CALF TRAINING

JASON E. COHEN

You hear it all the time: "My calves are never going to grow! It's genetics." The problem with that statement is that it's true—not the part about genetics but the part about the calves never growing. The reason is simple. When you say, "My calves will never grow," you put yourself in the frame of mind that they won't. I guarantee that if you change your way of thinking about calf training, you'll see new growth on your calves.

We can sit here and debate whether genetic predisposition determines your potential for building great calves, or we can get started on some hardcore calf training. The key to calf training can be summed up in one word—*intensity*. If you just go through the motions, up and down on the standing calf raise machine, your calves won't grow. Calves don't respond to low-intensity training because they're used to being worked all day, every day. Think about the way your calves bear the weight of your body every time you walk up stairs, get up from a chair, or walk out to your car. Therefore, it's important to raise the intensity level several notches when you train your calves.

Training with intensity involves having the mental stamina to break through certain pain barriers. For some reason—most likely due to the type of muscle fibers they contain—calves are extremely painful to train when you get to that last rep. Unfortunately, that's when they start growing. When they really start to burn, that's when you start counting reps.

TIPS FOR TRAINING YOUR CALVES

After you read this, you'll inevitably see people in the gym making the same mistakes you may be making now. The first involves footwear. Train your calves in flat-soled shoes. Even better, train them in your bare feet.

Second, your stance is very important. The most common mistake people make in training calves is to bend their knees too much. Remember, the goal is to take the quads out of the movement and isolate your calves. Slightly

One-leg standing calf raise.   Michael Ashley.

bent is all right, but I believe your legs should be as straight as you can get them. Position your feet with your heels a little wider than your toes. It's very important to put the pressure of the movement directly on your big toes. Having the weight there will really help you get a full contraction on every rep.

Another often-overlooked factor is stretching. I like to stretch my calves hard before training them. The calves are made up of the soleus and the gastrocnemius. To stretch the soleus, position yourself on a seated calf machine with no weight and stretch. To stretch the gastrocnemius, use the standing calf raise and stretch your heels to the ground. It's also a good idea to stretch your calves frequently between sets.

Finally, you want to concentrate on getting a full contraction on each and every rep. When you lower your heels, you'll feel as if you're

sliding off the calf machine. When you're at the top of the movement, you'll almost be standing on your big toes. You may have already noticed that the people who use huge weights and bounce on every rep have small calves.

WORKOUT 1

Exercise 1: High-rep standing calf raises

If you thought I was kidding about training intensity, you're about to be tested. The first movement will teach you what I mean about the mental stamina to break through pain barriers. Since most people like to do standing calf raises first, that's where you begin. In this case, however, you do a set of 50 reps. You perform all 50 reps consecutively but break down the set into 5 minisets of 10 reps. Set the standing calf raise machine with a weight that you can ordinarily use for 20 reps. Perform 10 slow, strict reps, followed by 10 bouncing reps—in which you literally bounce up and down. After that do 10 slow, strict reps; 10 bouncing reps; and, finally, 10 slow, strict reps. Do not rest between the strict reps and the bouncing reps. Just keep going until you complete 50 reps. If you don't feel like puking, you didn't go hard enough. Your calves should be burning; they should feel as if someone stuck a knife in them.

Ordinarily, I don't recommend bouncing on any exercise. As a matter of fact, I suggest a full, slow contraction on all your other calf exercises. The purpose of the bouncing reps here is to activate both the fast- and slow-twitch muscle fibers in your calves. In essence, you aren't really bouncing but, simply, increasing the tempo of the reps. Therefore, it's extremely important that you stretch your calves properly before starting this exercise.

Exercise 2: One-leg standing calf raises

This time you concentrate on one calf at a time. This exercise may seem a little strange

Standing calf raises.   Jody Friedman.

at first, but you'll really like it. Have you ever gone boating and discovered that your calves are really sore the next day? The soreness comes from balancing with the stabilizing muscles that you aren't used to working in the gym.

To perform this exercise, you'll need a calf block positioned near some uprights that you can use for support, or you can use the base of a power rack. Take a dumbbell that weighs about the same as the ones you generally use to begin your dumbbell curls. Stand on the block on your right leg with your toes on the edge and the dumbbell in your left hand. Rise on your toes and lower your heel slowly with the dumbbell at your side. You'll probably need to hold on to the uprights for balance. Once you master the motion, begin to move the dumbbell to the front of your body, holding it in a different position on each rep.

Count only the reps that burn. Once you start feeling pain, start counting. After you've completely worked your right calf, switch the dumbbell to your right hand and work the other calf. Perform 3 sets on each calf—counting only the reps that burn. Some people prefer to do this exercise at the beginning of their routine because it really works the stabilizing muscles. Many people have told me that their calves still feel fresh after they crush them on this movement.

Exercise 3: Donkey calf raises

Unfortunately, some gyms aren't equipped with a donkey calf raise machine. If your gym doesn't have one, you can do the same movement on a platform with your training partner on your back.

If you do have a donkey machine, do 3 drop sets. Use a relatively heavy weight for your first set and go to failure. Without resting, pull the pin and switch to a lighter weight and again go to failure. Then pull the pin a second time and go for a very light high-rep set. When you're through with the triple-drop set, you'll have tears in your eyes.

If you don't have a donkey machine, simply have your partner sit on your back while your toes are on a calf block. You can use a

Donkey calf raises.

weighted belt or have your partner hold some plates. On your first set go to failure and then have your partner drop the weight. Do another set to failure, then have your partner get off your back so you can do a final, high-rep set. People in the gym may look at you as if you're crazy, but just wait until your calves begin to explode with new growth.

WORKOUT 2: THE GAUNTLET

I recommend training calves twice a week. Don't do it as an afterthought, however. Treat your calves the way you treat your biceps, triceps, and chest. In other words, train them consistently and intensely.

Workout 2 is quick and painful. It consists of 2 giant sets. Most gyms have their calf machines situated next to one another. You'll need to occupy three different pieces of equipment. You can use the donkey calf machine, seated calf machine, standing calf machine, leg press calf raises, and/or the angled calf raise machine. If your gym has only two of these apparatuses, you can always substitute one-leg standing calf raises.

For this workout you perform the first exercise, immediately jump to the next piece of equipment, and, when you're finished, jump to the final piece of equipment. On each set choose a weight that you can handle for at least 10 reps, but always go to failure. It's necessary to set up all three machines before doing your giant set so you don't get a rest while you're loading plates. When you're finished with your first giant set, your calves will be burning so badly they'll be numb. That's what you want.

MY CALVES ARE KILLING ME!

There's no doubt that if you train your calves correctly with the necessary intensity, they'll grow. You'll be cursing me all the way to the water fountain and as you're trying to drive your stick-shift car home, but it will be worth it. The payoff for the tears rolling down your face when you finish a set of 50 reps is simple. First, you build up the mental stamina to break through pain barriers. Second, people who see your calves will comment on them. I don't know of a more impressive sight in the gym than a pair of stacked calves, and there's no mistaking the people who train their calves hard for those who just go through the motions.

Seated calf raises.   Boyer Coe.

Chapter 18

THE ULTIMATE PROGRAM
A DYNAMITE POWER-MASS-STRENGTH ROUTINE

BY C. S. SLOAN

I've never liked the term *hardgainer* because I believe a lot of people use it as an excuse for their inability to pack on strength and mass. "I can't" and "I won't" are common phrases in their vocabularies, and they often attribute the successes of other lifters to good genetics or drugs. For example, "If I was born with those parents and I could spend that much time eating and resting, I'd be that damn big as well."

The truth is that at least 98 percent of trainees have a very hard time gaining muscle. So, if you're a so-called hardgainer, you're not really in the minority, are you?

The first thing you need to do in your search for results is to get out of your head the idea that you're automatically at some disadvantage the rest of the world doesn't face. Start saying "I can" or, better yet, "I will." Then try out a program that's designed to stimulate muscle size and strength in the majority of trainees—average trainees like you.

If you've been lifting for a long time, you probably know the basic recommendations for

hard-gaining strength athletes. They usually go something like this:

1. Train very hard.
2. Train infrequently.
3. Use only basic, multijoint exercises.
4. Get plenty of rest between training sessions.
5. Eat lots of wholesome food, especially high-quality protein.

That pretty much sums it up.

Most of the routines include only 1 set per exercise per bodypart. Most of the sets are done for 6 to 12 reps and are taken to complete muscular failure. The following is a typical hardgainer routine. You perform it twice a week, say, on Monday and Thursday.

Squats	1 × 20
Dumbbell pullovers	1 × 10–12
Incline-bench presses	1 × 8–12
Pulldowns	1 × 8–12
Nautilus curls	1 × 8–12
Pushdowns	1 × 8–12

Barbell curl—start.   Christian Boeving.

Barbell curl—midrange.

Barbell curl—finish.

Such routines seem to work for a good many people. If you do the 20 squats like true 20-rep breathing squats, the program will definitely produce some gains in muscle tissue and all-around strength. Over the years, however, I've talked with a lot of people who don't get results from such programs, especially when they leave out the breathing squats. If that's you, don't worry. There are other effective approaches—fantastic routines that will add bulk to an average gainer's frame.

The program outlined below is probably one of the best for packing muscle and raw power on hard-gaining bodybuilders and strength athletes. It incorporates many techniques, including old-time methods such as the 5 × 5 system, heavy singles, and high-rep breathing exercises, plus more modern techniques such as negative reps, jump sets, partials, and drop sets. Give it a try for at least six weeks.

The ultimate program uses a threeway bodypart split, with three workouts performed on nonconsecutive days, usually Monday,

Wednesday, and Friday. Many average gainers find that they need even more rest. A one-on/two-off schedule is a good solution to the problem. Here's the way the cycle looks:

> Monday: Workout 1
> Tuesday and Wednesday: Off
> Thursday: Workout 2
> Friday and Saturday: Off
> Sunday: Workout 3
> Monday and Tuesday: Off
> Wednesday: Cycle begins again

WORKOUT 1

Chest and back

This routine is basic but brutal—just what average trainees need to make good gains. Start with some type of light warm-up for approximately 10 minutes—nothing hard or overly taxing, just enough to elevate your heart rate slightly and warm up your muscles. Light pedaling on the stationary bike or walking on the treadmill should do the job. You do the same type of warm-up for all three workouts.

After the warm-up, head over to everyone's favorite exercise—the bench press. Begin with one light warm-up set for 10 to 15 reps with nothing but the empty Olympic bar. Rest a minute or two and do a warm-up set of 5 with a weight that you can handle for about 10 reps.

For your work sets on the bench press you use the 5-4-3-2-1 method. Load the bar with whatever weight you can handle for about 5 hard repetitions and crank out your first work set of 5. After two to three minutes' rest, put 10 to 20 pounds on the bar and shoot for 4 reps. Rest a couple of minutes, then add another 10 to 20 pounds and shoot for 3. Repeat twice more, until you reach your final set of 1 all-out rep. Try to increase the amount of weight on each set every week, even if it's only by a couple of pounds. A lot of bodybuilders seem to have a fear of doing heavy singles, thinking they're only for powerlifters, but that isn't the case. You can also build a good deal of muscle if you use heavy singles properly and don't max out on every exercise at every workout.

After the bench presses come drop sets of inclines. Set up an incline bench and grab a pair of dumbbells that you know you can get 5 reps with. Then get two progressively lighter pairs of dumbbells and set them on the floor in front of you. For instance, if you took 80-pounders for your first pair, set a pair of 70s and a pair of 60s in front of them. Pick up the 80s, lean back on the bench, and try for 5 reps. When you reach 5, put down the dumbbells and immediately pick up the 70s and try for 5 more, then repeat with the 60-pounders.

Drop sets have long been a popular intensity technique, especially among the brigade of high-intensity lifters. They can work really well for hard-gaining bodybuilders, but, as with all intensity techniques, don't go overboard. One drop set will probably be plenty.

After a five-minute rest it's time for some heavy lat work. Use a big rowing movement, either bent-over barbell rows or T-bar rows,

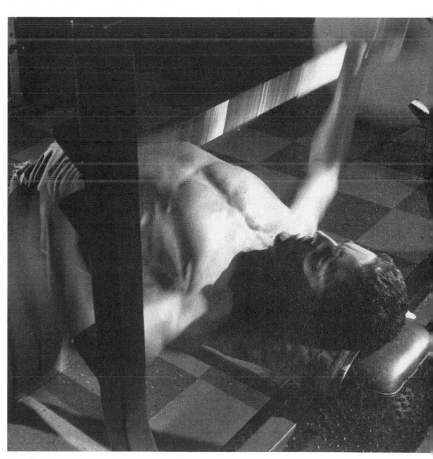

Bench press.

Bent-over barbell row—start.   Dave Tuttle.

Bent-over barbell row—midrange.

Bent-over barbell row—finish.

and use the 5 × 5 method, in which you do two progressively heavier warm-ups of 5 reps and then 3 sets with your top weight. For example, say the most you can do on bent-over barbell rows for 5 reps is 225 pounds. Your progression starts out with 1 set at 135 pounds for 5 reps and another at 185. On your first work set, shoot for 5 reps with 225. Rest a minute and repeat the 225, once again aiming for 5 reps. Rest a few more minutes and repeat. Once you can handle 5 reps easily on all 3 work sets, increase the weight at the next workout. It's as simple as it gets but extremely effective.

That's your only lat exercise. Take another five-minute rest, and then it's time to move on to some heavy barbell shrugs. You perform 5 to 6 progressively heavier sets of singles (that's right, only 1 rep!) until you reach a maximum attempt with whatever you can handle. Even though you're going heavy, make sure you use perfect form. Make each rep a full one by bringing the weight up as high as you can and really squeezing your trapezius muscles at the top before lowering the bar very slowly.

WORKOUT 2

Quads, hams, and lower back

Start with another light aerobic warm-up on the stationary bike or treadmill and get your blood flowing into those legs, then move to the squat rack. Use the 5 × 5 method, as described for rows in Workout 1. Squats are a hard exercise. If you don't get more than 2 or 3 reps on your last set, that's fine. Stick with it until 5 reps are fairly easy on all 3 sets, then add weight.

Don't wimp out on squats. Make sure you go deep on each rep, to where your hips are parallel to your knees. Squats and deadlifts are the most productive things you do in the gym. They're exceptional muscle-building tools for the average gainer.

Rest at least five minutes after your full-range squats. Then head over to the power rack for some partials. Set the pins so you start the movement about five to six inches from lockout. You're going to do singles, so warm

Steve Holman spots Jonathan Lawson's squat.

up over 5 to 6 progressively heavier 1-rep sets until you get to 95 percent of your 1-rep maximum (1RM).

The third and final exercise of the workout is 20-rep breathing deadlifts. After several light warm-ups, pick a weight that you'd usually use for 10 reps and instead go for 20. After each rep take at least two deep breaths. Once you reach about the 10th rep, you'll no doubt need five or six deep breaths to complete the set.

Twenty-rep deadlifts are absolutely brutal, no doubt about it, which is the reason most routines only recommend 1 work set (though I've done two in a workout often enough). They're also highly productive and can be the average gainer's best friend. Do not—I repeat, *do not*—leave them out of the program. They're an integral part of its success.

WORKOUT 3

Arms and shoulders

After your warm-up it's time for arm training and a technique known as jump sets, alternates, and power supersets. The exercises you alternate are barbell curls and close-grip bench presses, and you use the 5-4-3-2-1 method on both.

Warm up on the presses and curls with a couple of light sets using nothing but the bar. Load the bar with your 5-rep work weight and then crank out your first set. Rest two minutes, then move over to the close-grip bench presses for your first set of 5. Alternate back and forth in that manner, adding weight on each set and dropping one rep until you reach your max single on both exercises.

Jump sets work well because, when you activate the agonist muscles during a set and then do a set for the antagonist muscles, the antagonists can contract more intensely than if you hadn't done the agonist set. It's uncanny how well it works.

After the power arm training it's time to move on to shoulders and a seldom-used exercise, the push press. Position yourself in the squat rack and unrack the weight onto the

Overhead push press—start.

Overhead push press—finish.

fronts of your shoulders. Walk out of the rack and begin the set by initiating momentum with your legs, then explode the weight up above your head.

Do 4 sets of push presses to complete muscular failure. On your first set, pick a weight with which you think you can get 8 reps. On the 3 ensuing sets try to get at least 5 reps. Work these hard. You can do these behind your neck as well if you don't have shoulder problems.

That's it. The last workout is tough but not as demanding as the first two (although you may disagree after you try the push presses). Now you go home, rest, and get ready to start all over again in a couple of days.

THE SUM OF THE PARTS

Take as much rest between workouts as you need but try to stick to a fairly exact schedule. Don't get in the habit of taking off days just because you're too lazy to go to the gym.

If you haven't been working out for very long or if you've been doing a more traditional

hardgainer workout, go lighter for a week or two and give your body a chance to adjust to the routine. After that it's full steam ahead.

On the other hand, if you've been training with multiple workouts for a while, take at least two weeks off so your body can heal before you start this program.

Try to get as much rest as possible on your off days and be sure to eat plenty of wholesome food, including complex carbs and protein.

Put it all together, and it's one power-packed program for the hardgainer in all of us—simple, no-nonsense, and, most important, highly effective.

ULTIMATE MASS-POWER-AND-STRENGTH ROUTINE

Workout 1: Chest and Back

Bench presses	5 × 5, 4, 3, 2, 1
Incline dumbbell presses	1 × 5 × triple drop
Bent-over barbell rows or	
T-bar rows	5 × 5
Shrugs	5–6 × 1

Deadlift—start.

Deadlift—finish.

Workout 2: Quads, Hams, and Lower Back

Squats	5 × 5
Partial squats	5–6 × 1
Deadlifts	1 × 20

Workout 3: Arms and Shoulders

Barbell curls (alternated with)	5 × 5, 4, 3, 2, 1
Close-grip bench presses	5 × 5, 4, 3, 2, 1
Push presses	4 × failure

Chapter 19

HARDGAINER CALL TO ARMS

BY STUART MCROBERT

Most trainees spend great chunks of their lives thinking about what they should be doing to improve their training, their diets, their supplementation. A lot of them, however, actually never get around to doing the kind of training they need. As a result they never do what will satisfy them most—develop the body and strength they crave. Successful muscle building is all about progressively adding poundages to lifts performed consistently and with good form.

You must live to add weight to each exercise. How many people actually focus on that goal? How many people in the gym where you train are instead concerned with the latest designer supplement or the latest gossip? When you think about it, it's utterly crazy. The result is that most of the people who make decent gains are those with terrific genetics or those who are stupid enough to take drugs.

Most people who read about abbreviated and basics-first training make only minor changes in their programs. They tinker a bit here and there, but they never really make radical changes. Unless your training is going extremely well, start the program described in this chapter. It's designed to make you bigger and stronger all over. It's not a program for fat loss or to bring up a lagging bodypart. Most trainees don't need to fine-tune their physiques or get ready for a contest. Most of them just need more muscles.

Don't read through the program and find fault with it or try to improve it. Have faith and just follow it. A training schedule doesn't have to be perfect to work. For at least 10 weeks just follow the program exactly as I describe it. Start now. Don't put it off until next month or next year.

Before you start, take seven days off from weight training to give yourself a chance to recover from any overtraining you may have incurred.

Seated dumbbell presses.   Jim Shiebler.

THE PROGRAM

Train only two days a week—Monday and Thursday, Tuesday and Friday, or Wednesday and Saturday. Choose the days when you're most likely to perform at your best. If, for example, Mondays are your toughest days at work, don't train on Mondays. You need to be able to go to bed an hour earlier on your workout days to get in extra muscle-building sleep.

Perform two different routines, alternating them. You train twice a week but do each routine only once a week. As with all good routines, these are short.

Workout 1

Squats or leg presses	2 × 8
Bench presses or parallel bar dips	2 × 6
Pulldowns	2 × 6
Grip work (see this page)	
Crunches	2 × 15

Workout 2

Trap bar or stiff-legged deadlifts	2 × 6
Seated dumbbell presses	2 × 8
Barbell curls	2 × 8
Standing calf raises	2 × 15
Side bends	2 × 12
Grip work of your choice	

These two workouts are the work sets. Warm up before each exercise. For the biggest exercises do two or three progressive warm-ups, but for the smallest a single warm-up set will suffice. For example, your warm-up sets for the bench press could be 135 × 10, 185 × 6, and 220 × 6 to precede 2 work sets of 245 × 6. For the barbell curls, though, a single warm-up set of 60 × 8 is adequate to precede work sets of 90 × 8. Begin each workout with five minutes of low-intensity stationary cycling, skiing, climbing, or skipping—until you break a sweat.

For the grip work in the first workout do holds, preferably with a thick bar. Take the loaded bar off the power rack pins as if you

Greg Blount.

were doing the top part of a deadlift. Find a weight that you can hold for exactly 60 seconds. Rest for one minute and then hold the same weight again. Your target is to hold the bar for 30 seconds on your second hold. *Hold* is actually the wrong word—try to crush it. Add a little weight each week, but make sure you hold for the full 60 seconds.

Take it relatively easy for the first two weeks to familiarize yourself with the exercises and practice good form. Push quite hard in the third week and then start pulling out all the stops in the fourth. Thereafter you must push very hard at each session. Try your utmost to add a pound or more to each exercise each week.

Because you do the same reps for each set, the first set isn't as intense as the second. Rest for a few minutes between sets—just long enough for you to do justice to the next set. When you can't make all of the reps on the second set of a given exercise, don't increase the weight until you can. If you add weight too quickly or too often, it will be your downfall.

Here's a sample progressive deadlift scheme, including the heaviest warm-up set.

> Week 1: 225 × 6, 250 × 6, 250 × 6
> Week 2: 225 × 6, 260 × 6, 260 × 6
> Week 3: 225 × 6, 270 × 6, 270 × 6
> Week 4: 240 × 6, 275 × 6, 275 × 6
> Week 5: 240 × 6, 280 × 6, 280 × 6
> Week 6: 240 × 6, 285 × 6, 285 × 6
> Week 7: 250 × 6, 290 × 6, 290 × 6
> Week 8: 250 × 6, 290 × 6, 290 × 6
> Week 9: 250 × 6, 292.5 × 6, 292.5 × 6
> Week 10: 250 × 6, 295 × 6, 295 × 6

Possible modifications

While some people respond well to different rep counts for a movement, others don't. If, for example, you know that you don't respond well to sets of 8 but do respond to sets of 15 to 20, use the rep count that works best for you. "Best for you" is whatever lets you add weight regularly. If you don't know what's best, stick with the target reps suggested above.

You may also need to adjust the exercises used in the two workouts. Some people find it very productive to do squats and deadlifts on different days because squats and deadlifts are overlapping exercises, meaning they work a lot of the same muscles. Other people, however, do better if they put both movements in one workout. That way the glutes, lower back, and thighs get one hard session a week and have a full seven days to recover. So if your deadlift or squat poundages grind to a halt, put the two exercises into one routine. (If you're doing leg presses and stiff-legged deadlifts, though, you may find it doesn't make much difference. There's nowhere near as much overlap in those two movements.)

The same approach applies to the bench presses or parallel bar dips in Workout 1 and the overhead dumbbell presses in Workout 2. If, when you are deep into the program, you find that your poundages aren't increasing, try putting the two exercises into the same workout so your shoulders get a full week's rest. When you rearrange your schedule, make sure you maintain the same number of exercises in

each workout. If you move the dumbbell presses to Workout 1, switch the pulldowns to Workout 2.

You may also need to use different exercises because you don't have the right equipment. If you don't have a pulldown unit available, substitute a prone row, chin, or one-arm dumbbell row.

TECHNIQUE

Good form is the bedrock of training success. Without it your program is doomed to failure because sooner or later you'll injure yourself. What is good form? Well, it's not what you see in most gyms. Because I can't be with you to check your form or determine whether whoever advises you knows what he or she is talking about, I can only recommend that you get my new book. I know that sounds commercial and self-serving, but I honestly can't recommend any other book. Please get a copy of *Weight-Training Technique* and follow the advice in it so you can look forward to years of injury-free, successful bodybuilding.

NUTRITION AND REST

Don't undermine the huge potential of the program by failing to give yourself adequate nutrition and rest. You must eat a high-quality diet packed with enough nutritious food to grow on. Follow it up by getting to sleep early enough that you wake each morning of your own volition.

EFFORT

None of this will matter unless you really push yourself in the gym. If you loaf, you'll make minimal or no progress. To stimulate increases in strength, you must push yourself very hard on a consistent basis.

THE WRAP-UP

After you follow this program for 10 weeks, you may discover that you've made more progress than you did over the previous six months. When that happens, you'll know what productive muscle building is all about.

You'll get stronger, and your muscles will grow. You'll relish your training. You'll be fully rested between workouts. You'll pour maximum effort into each session. You'll see yourself progressing. This in turn will fire you up to train harder and better, and thus you'll gain more. You'll be sore and a bit tired on your off days, but you won't be totally wiped out. Your appetite will increase because your body is growing and needs more sustenance. In short, you'll have found the Holy Grail of successful drug-free weight training.

You don't have to stop at 10 weeks. If the program is still working for you, keep doing it. You could get as much as six months of small but steady gains. That will add up to substantial improvement.

Now that you know how to train, put the knowledge to work. Deliver the unrelenting dedication. Get growing and become walking testimony to the enormous effectiveness of abbreviated, drug-free training.

Michael Hernando.

Chapter 20

TEAM UNIVERSE CHAMPION WORKOUTS

BY LONNIE TEPER

MICHAEL HERNANDO

With Earl Snyder, who had two consecutive victories under his belt, leading the way in a tough Bantamweight class, rookie Michael Hernando was just hoping to get a peek from the judges in New York at the '96 NPC Team Universe Championships. Top five would be dandy, said the 26-year-old from Holmdel, New Jersey. But when Hernando, the son of a surgeon, showed up with a 5'5", 142-pound shredded, symmetrical package, it appeared that he would be the one operating on the competition at the prestigious national event.

Folks who attended the '95 Natural Eastern Classic weren't a bit surprised that Hernando was able to best the rest at the Team Universe. After all, they saw him win the Overall, and how often does a Bantamweight outmuscle the other class winners to become the real heavyweight in bodybuilding?

Hernando, who was raised in New Jersey, was a standout athlete in high school, earning all-state honors with his brother in doubles tennis competition. The 125-pound skinny kid was also powerful enough to win the district championship when he left the tennis court for a wrestling mat.

Although Hernando, who's of Filipino descent, tinkered with weights in high school, he really didn't spend much time training until he entered Rutgers University, where his buddies liked to pump iron. Most of his efforts, however, took place in the classroom, and in 1993 he earned a degree in biology with honors. After that he began having consistent dates with the weights.

Hernando's first show was the '94 AAU New Jersey, where he finished second in the Short class. A year later he returned to avenge his defeat but ended up one slot lower, in third. "It was tough in the AAU because I was so thin for my height," he says. "Most of the guys weighed 170, 180."

Michael's fortunes changed when he switched to the NPC and entered Bob Bonham's famed Natural Eastern Classic. And the rest, as they say, is history.

Michael Hernando.

Hernando trains at the Powerhouse Gym in Old Bridge, a 15-minute drive from his home. In the off-season he gets up to 165 pounds, and he admits his days as a Bantamweight are numbered. "I think at my height I have to be a Lightweight," Hernando says. He also believes he started making significant gains after his appearances at the Mr. New Jersey, when he began taking supplements.

"I never really believed in them before," he says, "and just thought following a healthy diet would do it. Then I started using things like creatine and protein shakes—and I also changed my workout cycle from hitting each bodypart twice a week to once a week—and I really started to make some gains."

Hernando doesn't have any aspirations to stand on a pro bodybuilding stage. He has applied to medical school and is currently working as an assistant in his father's office, as he wants to stand in for Pop when Franklin Hernando, M.D., turns in his scalpel. In the meantime, though, Michael will continue to do some slicing of his own on the physique ward.

MICHAEL HERNANDO'S RAZOR-SHARP TRAINING

Unless he's training to failure, he pyramids weights on each successive set.

Day 1: Chest and Biceps
Chest

Bench presses (warm-up)	1 × 10, 3 × 5
(work sets)	1 × 5, 2 × 5 or failure
Incline dumbbell presses	3 × 10 or failure
Incline machine presses*	3 × failure

*No more than 10 reps.

Biceps

Barbell curls (warm-up)	2 × 10
(work sets)	3 × 6 or failure
Seated dumbbell curls	3 × 10 or failure

Day 2: Quads and Calves
Quads

Smith machine squats (warm-up)	1 × 10, 3 × 5, 1 × 10
(work sets)	2 × failure
Hack squats	3 × 6–10
Leg extensions	3 × 10

Calves

Standing calf raises	3 × 15
Seated calf raises	3 × 15

Day 3: Abs and Traps
Abs

Seated weighted crunches	2 × 20
Kneeling weighted rope crunches	2 × 20
Hanging leg raises	2 × 20
Decline situps	2 × 20
Crunches	2 × 20
Side crunches	2 × 20

Traps

Barbell shrugs	6 × 10

Day 4: Shoulders and Triceps
Shoulders

Military presses (warm-up)	3 × 5
(work sets)	1 × 5, 2 × failure
Dumbbell presses	3 × failure
Lateral raises	3 × failure
Bent-over lateral raises	3 × failure

Triceps

Cable pushdowns (warm-up)	3 × 5
(work sets)*	3 × 10
Cable overhead extensions	3 × 10

*To failure on last set.

Day 5: Back and Hamstrings
Back

One-arm dumbbell rows (warm-up)	3 × 10
(work sets)*	2 × 10
T-bar rows	3 × 10
Lat pulldowns	3 × 10

Hamstrings

Seated leg curls	3 × 10
Hyperextensions	3 × 15

*To failure on last set.

Days 6 and 7: Off

CHRIS FAILDO

Like Middleweight champ Johnny Stewart, Chris Faildo made his mark in bodybuilding long before his success at the '96 NPC Team Universe Championships. Born and raised in Honolulu, Faildo earned his nickname, the "Hawaiian Hurricane," during a remarkable 12-year career, blowing away opponents in both tested and nontested events.

Bodybuilding historians remember Faildo as the Lightweight winner at the '85 Teen Nationals, although those who don't follow the sport as closely might only recollect that Shawn Ray won the Light Heavyweight class

Chris Faildo.

that year and Shane DiMora was the Middleweight champ.

Likewise, a lot of people forget that it was the drug-free Faildo who came out on top in the Lightweight class at the '93 USA Championships, an event that featured one of the most powerful Heavyweight lineups of all time, led by eventual victor Chris Cormier.

After placing second in the World Amateur Championships in 1995, Faildo made it three for three at the Team Universe, scoring another unanimous victory in a supreme class that once again included the spectacular Steve Holland, another former USA class winner.

Unlike the other '96 Team Universe champs, Faildo wasn't a high school sensation on the football field or in the wrestling arena. In fact, at 5'4″ and 105 pounds he was a Barney Fife look-alike and a mainstay of the school band as master of the clarinet, an instrument he plays to this day as a member of the 111th Army National Guard band.

Chris tried to make it as a baseball player, but he was tinier than the bat, so in his sophomore year he decided it was time to hit the weights and keep the bullies off his narrow back. The strategy worked. Training at Timmy Leong's gym, Faildo packed on 40 pounds of muscle over the next two and a half years, and after finishing a dismal tenth in his junior year, he won the Mr. High School bodybuilding title at Farrington High as a senior. Immediately after that the tough guys became his buddies. "I was never real strong with my lifts, but I was strong-minded and I won the show," he says proudly.

A year later he took the Teen Nationals division, but when he couldn't take home the state Open title after two tries, Chris decided he needed a break and spent four years away from the stage before coming back to win the Hawaii Championships in 1992.

Despite his frustration over the consecutive losses at the Hawaii, Faildo never even considered using bodybuilding drugs, which would have put a lock on the trophy he longed for. "It was a tough four years, keeping my mind focused," he says, "but I was never tempted to take drugs. I wanted to be different—successful and different.

"The key for a natural bodybuilder is what he does outside of the gym. Anybody can get in there and train, but what I do outside of the gym, nobody knows. It's having a total dedication to the sport while balancing my life between bodybuilding, family, and work."

Although Faildo was a twig in his younger days, that didn't present a problem for his wife, Tracy, who fell for his sweet lines when they were classmates in junior high school. "She was my first and last girlfriend, and I was her first and last boyfriend," Faildo says. "And we've been together ever since. We got married four years ago."

Faildo is as dedicated as anyone in the sport today. In fact, some may think his need for extreme regimentation qualifies him for a one-way ticket to a rubber room. "I am a fanatic," he admits. "Every Friday is prep night for me. I plan my entire week. Saturday is cooking day; I'll cook everything for the upcoming week. My clothes have to be ironed for the whole week and so forth. Once I start my diet, there's no cheating; in the off-season I cheat only on Sundays."

Faildo, who got up to 192 pounds during his last off-season, takes in anywhere from 6,000 to 7,000 calories per day, then cuts back to 3,000, slowly tapering down over a four-month period. He believes that the natural bodybuilder must train intensely and strictly but be aware of the critical need for recuperation. "I feel a two-days-on/one-day-off schedule is the best type of program for the noncompetitor," he says. "Even now, when preparing for a show, I make sure I get two days of rest per week."

Rest is a term that should be eliminated from the Faildo vocabulary, however, since it seems impossible that he gets any with a schedule that includes his duties as Hawaii's main distributor for Twinlab products, his job in a family-owned printing business, and the weekly National Guard meetings, in addition to his obligations as a bodybuilder and husband.

Although the United States team passed on the '96 IFBB World Amateur Championships in Jordan due to the political climate in the Middle East, Faildo will be back at the

Team Universe in 1997. If he does get to the Worlds again and earn his pro card, don't expect him to be champing at the bit to get on a pro stage. "I will never compete as a pro unless they change the rules," he says. "I want mandatory random testing for all drugs year-round. If that doesn't happen, I will see if there's a way to still compete as an amateur; if not, my competition days will be over."

Shoot, Chris, even if they are, I'm sure you'll find a way to fill your day.

CHRIS FAILDO'S KILLER TRAINING

"The day starts off with my first of three cardio sessions at 4 A.M.," Faildo says. "I either jog for four miles or ride the stationary bike for 45 minutes. I prefer to jog—this seems to be the trick that gets my glutes striated. I ride the Lifecycle only when my quads feel worn down from a previous leg workout. My next cardio session is done on the treadmill for 30 minutes prior to my workout, which starts at 3 P.M.

Now comes the fun part—balls-to-the-wall intense training for an hour. Then it's back for another 30 minutes of cardio on the Stairmaster. Some people may criticize me for the amount of time spent doing all that boring cardio, but it's what enables me to obtain that rock-hard look I'm known for on stage."

Day 1: Off
45-minute cardio session

Day 2: Chest, Triceps, and Calves
Chest

Incline barbell or dumbbell presses	4 × 8–10
Flat-bench dumbbell presses	3 × 8–10
Incline dumbbell flyes	3 × 8–10
Weighted dips	3 × 8–10
Pullovers	3 × 8–10

Triceps

Seated EZ-curl bar French presses	3 × 8–10
Pushdowns	3 × 8–10
Kickbacks	3 × 8–10

Calves

Standing calf raises	4 × 8–10
Seated calf raises	4 × 8–10

Day 3: Back, Forearms, and Abs
Back

Pullups	4–5 × 8–10
Bent-over reverse barbell rows	3 × 8–10
Low-pulley rows	3 × 8–10
Deadlifts	4 × 8–10

Forearms

Seated reverse curls on bench	3 × 12–15
Hammer curls	3 × 12–15

Abs
Assorted exercises

Day 4: Quads, Hamstrings, and Calves
Quads

Squats or leg presses	4 × 12–15
Hack squats	4 × 12–15
Leg extensions	3 × 12–15
Lunges	3 × 12–15

Hamstrings

Lying leg curls	4 × 15–20
Standing leg curls	3 × 15–20
Stiff-legged deadlifts	3 × 15–20
Side lunges	3 × 15–20

Calves

Donkey calf raises	4 × 8–10
Leg press toe raises	4 × 8–10

Day 5: Off
Two 45-minute cardio sessions

Day 6: Shoulders, Traps, Biceps, and Abs
Shoulders

Behind-the-neck barbell presses	4 × 8–10
Seated dumbbell presses	4 × 8–10
Lateral raises	3 × 8–10
Bent-over laterals	3 × 8–10

Traps

Dumbbell shrugs	4 × 6–8
Reverse barbell shrugs	4 × 6–8

Biceps

Standing straight-bar or EZ-curl bar curls	4 × 8–10
Seated incline curls	3 × 8–10
Cable concentration curls	3 × 8–10

Abs
Assorted exercises

Day 7: Repeat Day 2 Workout

JOHNNY STEWART

If Johnny Stewart's Overall victory at the '96 NPC Team Universe shocked folks, they must not have been payin' too much attention to this contest for the previous two years—or to his award-winning career in the industry over the past decade. Stewart, a thick-as-a-brick 5'4", 173-pounder from Charlotte, North Carolina, made his debut at the inaugural Team Universe in 1994 with a strong fourth-place finish in the Middleweights. He came back in '95 to finish behind only class and Overall winner Yohnnie Shambourger, who went on to become the United States team's only victor at the ensuing World Amateur Championships.

Johnny Stewart.

The 34-year-old Stewart showed up in New York in his all-time-best shape, which is saying something considering the cat has showstopping calves and a Lee Haney–like pectoral region. Even with such veteran standouts as Harry Jonassaint in the class, Stewart breezed to a unanimous victory before overpowering the rest of the class winners and duplicating Shambourger's feat of showing that a Middleweight can have the top physique on a bodybuilding stage.

Stewart scored his initial athletic success on a wrestling mat, when he took the North Carolina state title in the 132-pound class while representing Scotland High School in Laurenberg. Johnny then spent a couple of seasons tossing opponents around at Elizabeth City State University, but he didn't expend too much energy in the weight room because, as he puts it, "I put on muscle too easily, and I didn't want to limit my mobility."

When Stewart finally concentrated his efforts on the iron, he became an immediate success in both bodybuilding and powerlifting. In 1987 he won the National Drug Free title with a 600-pound deadlift; at a 1990 meet, he benched 390 pounds in a meet at a bodyweight of 164.

He also won the first physique contest he ever entered, the '84 Mr. North Carolina, as a 151-pound Lightweight. He went on to win just about every title in his home state, and, after seeing that the new breed of powerlifters were matching his best marks with their open lifts, he decided it was time to concentrate solely on flexing instead of lifting.

In 1989 Stewart won the Lightweight class at the NPC Tennessee Championships, then followed that up with a class triumph at Peter Potter's renowned Southern States Championships. A year later he took the division at the Eastern Seaboard Championships, and in 1992 he really put his name on the bodybuilding map by besting everyone in the 154-pound class at the Junior Nationals.

"I was doing damage as a Lightweight," Stewart says, "but I was losing muscle to make the weight class. When I competed at the Juniors, I knew it would be my last year as a Lightweight—I was looking my best around

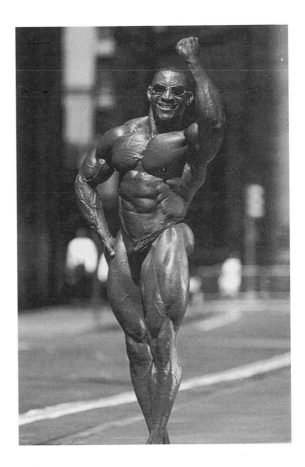

165, and I would suffer down to 154 to make the class."

Stewart returned to the Southern States in 1994 to test the waters as a Middleweight and proved to be a major success, finishing behind Dexter Jackson, who also copped the Overall crown.

Stewart, who might hold the NPC record for having the most children (six) before reaching the age of 35, said going up a class was his best career move to date. "I'm actually competing closer to my natural bodyweight, and it's easier for me to make the weight— I was actually at my competition weight a month prior to the contest this year. The highest I've ever gotten up to is 185.

"I don't do any cardio—haven't done any in three years—because I have a really fast metabolism," he continued. "I just keep a close eye on my calories. In the off-season I take in 5,500 calories a day. I break it down this way: 208 grams of protein, 680 grams of carbs, and anywhere from 40 to 60 grams of fat. Precontest I start out with 3,500 calories daily, with my protein intake the same. I drop 100 grams off my carbs and the fat goes down to a minimum. I can get ready for a show in 6 weeks, but I usually taper down over a 12-week period."

Stewart, who's definitely looking to earn a pro card, believes his calves, back, and hamstrings are his best bodyparts but says he now "brings the total package to the table" when he hits the stage. If he has a weakness, it's his quads, and he says he needs to bring them up prior to hitting a pro stage.

The irrepressible Stewart trains at Ric Flair's Gold's Gym in Charlotte and feels he's just at the beginning of a successful career. He sees himself as a hard 180-to-185-pounder who will, like Lee Labrada, be able to hold his own against anyone at the next level. Even the thought of facing five-time Mr. Olympia

Dorian Yates doesn't make Stewart doubt his chances as a pro. "I'll stand next to anyone," the confident Stewart says proudly. "As Ernest T. Bass [a character from *The Andy Griffith Show*] said, 'You can't make a silk purse out of a sow's ear'—a person who has good genetics doesn't need to take steroids. If you combine good genetics with proper training, learn smart nutritional habits, and be patient, the natural competitor can compete against the drug users."

Stewart has accomplished all of his feats as a powerlifter, bodybuilder, and baby maker while putting in a full workweek as a supervisor at Averitt Express, a trucking firm in Charlotte. His schedule is full, and so are his muscles.

JOHNNY STEWART'S CHAMPIONSHIP TRAINING

Stewart trains on a two-days-on/one-day-off schedule, using the following bodypart split. He works his calves and abs before and after each workout, alternating exercises for the two on each set.

Calves

Standing, seated, and donkey calf raises	4 × 8

Abs

Machine crunches, hanging side twists, and regular crunches	3 × 25

Day 1: Chest and Biceps
Chest

Flat-bench presses	7 × 6
Close-grip bench presses	2 × 6
Flat-bench flyes	4 × 6
Incline barbell presses	4 × 6
Incline dumbbell presses	3 × 8
Weighted dips	3 × 12
Hammer Strength close-grip bench presses*	3 × 12, 8, 6
Hammer Strength incline presses	3 × 12
Cable crossovers	3 × 25

Biceps

Straight-bar curls	3 × 12

Preacher curls	3 × 12
Hammer Strength preacher curls	3 × 12
Alternate dumbbell curls	3 × 12

Day 2: Quads
Squats*	5 × 20
Leg extensions*	10 × 20
Leg presses*	5 × 20
Hack squats*	4 × 20

*Add weight on each successive set.

Day 3: Off

Day 4: Hamstrings and Back
Hamstrings
Stiff-legged deadlifts	3 × 20
Leg curls	4 × 20
One-leg leg curls	3 × 20
Seated leg curls	3 × 20

Back
Seated rows	4 × 12
Pulldowns to front	3 × 12
Pullups	3 × 20
T-bar rows	3 × 12
Dumbbell rows	3 × 12
Bent-over rows	3 × 12
Hammer Strength seated rows	3 × 12
Hammer Strength front pulldowns	3 × 12

Day 5: Triceps and Shoulders
Shoulders
Dumbbell lateral raises	3 × 12
Upright rows	3 × 12
Behind-the-neck presses	3 × 12
Seated dumbbell presses	3 × 12
Dumbbell front raises	3 × 12
Dumbbell shrugs	3 × 12

Triceps
Pushdowns	4 × 12
Rope pushdowns	4 × 12
French presses	3 × 12
Nose breakers	3 × 12
Dumbbell kickbacks	3 × 12

Day 6: Off

Day 7: Repeat Day 1

MILTON HOLLOWAY

After finishing second to Overall winner Ronnie Coleman in the Light Heavyweight class at the '94 NPC Team Universe Championships, Milton Holloway hoped to find a smooth path to the title in 1995. When the 5'9", 196-pounder from Newcastle, Delaware, missed his nonstop flight to Chicago and had to take two planes to get to the event, however, his problems were just beginning.

First, he arrived late and barely made it to the weigh-in. Then, because of the added stress due to his last-minute itinerary changes, the 29-year-old was holding more water than anticipated. Milton feels these mishaps contributed greatly to another runner-up finish; this time he lost out to Darrell Monson in a close decision.

Fortunately for Holloway, and unfortunately for Monson and the rest of the Light Heavies at the '96 show, New York is less than a two-hour drive from Holloway's abode, so he

Milton Holloway.

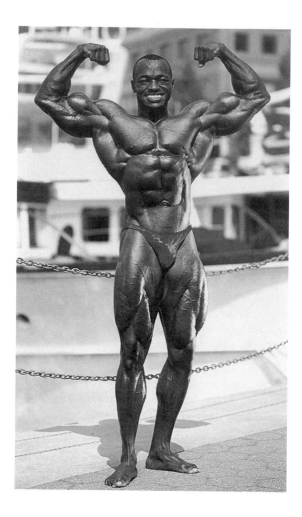

stepped on stage at the Tribeca Performing Arts Center well rested and well conditioned—well enough, in fact, to score a three-point victory over Monson to retaliate for his defeat of 1995.

Holloway, a Delaware native whose idol was Tony Atlas, not Charles Atlas, began lifting weights because he envisioned a career as a professional wrestler. He didn't compete in that sport in high school, though, because the coaches wanted him to lose weight, not add poundage.

After seeing the way Milton's physique responded to the weight program he started in his parents' basement when he was 15 years old, his friends encouraged him to compete in bodybuilding. Certainly he had the advantage of his genetics, which include tremendous arms, legs, and back, along with a small waist that has some folks calling him a smaller version of Vince Taylor or Flex Wheeler.

Holloway's initial contest was the '89 AAU Tri-State in New Jersey, at which he won the Novice competition and took second in his class in the Men's Open. Eventually, he went on to win the Natural Eastern Classic in 1993, the largest drug-tested contest on the East Coast. A year later he added the Mid-Atlantic Natural Classic to his bodybuilding résumé.

Milton spent one year at Norfolk State University in Virginia after high school and currently works full time as a chemical operator in Newcastle, a position he's held for the past nine years. Because of an extremely fast metabolism, he needs to diet for only five weeks prior to a contest. At the time of this interview he had more on his mind than just bodybuilding, as he was anticipating his wedding to Deborah, his girlfriend of six years.

Holloway trains Monday through Friday at either the Gold's Gym in Wilmington or The Training Center in Newcastle, using a five-days-on/two-days-off program in the off-season, when he gets up to around the 220-pound mark.

When asked what advice he had to give to natural competitors, he said, "I would say train to get quality muscle. When you have quality muscle, that stays with you when you diet down for a show, whereas the person who takes steroids gets bloated and loses a lot of muscle he thought he had when he starts dropping weight for the contest."

Although the soft-spoken Holloway doesn't believe that he's particularly strong, consider the fact that the folks at the gym had to order 180-pound dumbbells so he could do his flat-bench flyes. And his 450-pound squats for reps don't exactly qualify him for Weakling of the Month.

He admits he's trained his calves like mad, without much success, over the years, and, because he will not fill his body with chemicals, he doesn't foresee a grand career as a pro if he gets that far. "I would probably do one pro show, just to see where I would finish," Holloway says, "but with all the stuff these guys are taking today, there's no way I could compete with them."

Don't worry about that, Milton. You're doing just fine the way you are.

MILTON HOLLOWAY'S OFF-SEASON TRAINING

Note that he increases weight on each successive set on most exercises.

Day 1: Chest and Arms
Chest

Flat-bench dumbbell presses	4 × 10
Incline dumbbell presses	4 × 10
Icarian pec deck	4 × 10

Biceps

Standing straight-bar curls	4 × 10
Seated alternate dumbbell curls	4 × 10
Preacher curls	4 × 10

Triceps

Lying triceps extensions	4 × 10
Pushdowns	4 × 10
Kickbacks	4 × 10

Day 2: Legs and Calves
Quads

Squats	4 × 10
Leg presses	4 × 10
Leg extensions	3 × 10

Hamstrings

One-leg leg curls	4 × 10
Lying leg curls	4 × 10

Calves

Seated calf raises*	4 × 20–50
Standing calf raises	4 × 20

*Start with 20 reps and increase by 10 on each successive set.

Day 3: Abs, Calves, and Cardio

Day 4: Back and Shoulders
Back

Pullups	4 × 10–20
Bent-over rows	4 × 10
One-arm rows	4 × 10
Reverse seated pulley rows	4 × 10

Shoulders

Smith machine front presses	4 × 10

Dumbbell front raises	3 × 10
Reverse pec deck rear delts	4 × 10

Day 5: Legs

Vertical leg presses	4 × 10
Hack squats	4 × 10
Stiff-legged deadlifts	4 × 10

ROBERT WASHINGTON

Robert Washington's buddies at Olympic Gym in San Antonio, Texas, didn't have to remind him that Skip La Cour, who bested Washington in the Heavyweight class at the '95 Team Universe, would be back in the lineup in '96 after placing sixth at the World Amateur Championships.

"I read all of Skip's articles in *Ironman*," says the 34-year-old Washington, "and he wrote that he was going to do the Team

Robert Washington.

Universe again, so that was more than enough to keep me really focused."

Unlike '95, when Washington came in off the mark after competing three times in six weeks, the Savannah, Georgia, native concentrated only on the Team Universe battle, and it showed. Although he thinks he was much sharper 24 hours prior to the contest Washington breezed through the division; his powerful 5'10", 227-pound physique produced a unanimous victory.

Washington should be used to feeling powerful. After making a name for himself in high school and at East Carolina University as a hard-hitting outside linebacker, he began powerlifting in 1984 and swiftly became one of the best in the country.

He finished behind only five-time world-record holder Ed Coan in the '86 Senior Nationals, with best lifts of 525 in the bench press, 750 in the squat, and 830 in the deadlift at a bodyweight of 219.5 pounds. Coan was

both his inspiration and his nemesis—because Washington's squat was about 250 pounds short of Coan's, Robert decided it was time to leave the lifting stage for the posing dais.

His first show was the '93 Metroplex in Dallas, where he finished second as a 216-pound Heavyweight. He scored his first victory at the World Classic in his hometown of San Antonio a year later. Robert admits he cheated on his diet when preparing for the '95 T.U., "going off it for 24 hours, then getting back on it, and so forth. I was just worn out and didn't come in sharp."

This time around he started his diet 12 weeks out and for the most part stuck to it. Because his off-season weight rose to 254 pounds, Robert added two one-hour sessions on the stationary bike to his training. "I normally do about 30 minutes of cardio in the off-season," he says, "but I had to really come down, so I did cardio when I first got up at four in the morning and before I went to bed at night."

Washington, who sported the thickest back in the contest, was happy that he beat La Cour this time around, thrilled with the unanimous win, but not totally satisfied with his performance. "I overcarbed and spilled over," he says. "If I was two, three pounds of water lighter, I think I could have given Johnny [Stewart] a real go for the Overall title."

Robert shouldn't have had much trouble getting up for those early dates with the bike, as his daughter, who was born two months before the contest, provided the shrills—er, the tunes—folks enjoy listening to while burning those calories. Robert and his wife, Kim, also have of a two-year-old son. Kim's 13-year-old son, Brenden, is a member of the Washington household as well.

Even though Washington put away his powerlifting gloves four years ago, he still puts away powerlifting numbers in his current workouts. He benches 625 in the off-season, gets 5 reps at 750 in the squat and has recorded a 450 bent-over row.

One thing is for certain: Other competitors may beat Robert Washington, but they won't overpower him!

ROBERT WASHINGTON'S OFF-SEASON TRAINING

Washington uses a six-days-on/one-day-off schedule in both his off-season and precontest training. For the precontest cycle he increases the reps and lowers the weight a bit. Here's a typical off-season program.

Day 1: Chest and Triceps
Chest

Bench presses	4 × 12, 10, 8, 6
Incline presses	4 × 12, 10, 8, 6
Decline presses	4 × 12, 10, 8, 6

Triceps

Pushdowns	4 × 12, 10, 8, 6
Close-grip bench presses	1 × 12, 10, 8, 6
Dips	4 × 12, 10, 8, 6
Kickbacks	4 × 12, 10, 8, 6

Day 2: Legs and Calves
Legs

Squats	4 × 12, 10, 8, 6
Leg presses	4 × 12, 10, 8, 6
Leg extensions	4 × 12, 10, 8, 6

Calves

Standing calf raises	4 × 12, 10, 8, 6
Donkey calf raises	4 × 12, 10, 8, 6
Seated calf raises	4 × 12, 10, 8, 6

Day 3: Back and Biceps
Back

Lat pulldowns	4 × 12, 10, 8, 6
Bent-over rows	4 × 12, 10, 8, 6
One-arm lat pulls	4 × 12, 10, 8, 6
Wide-grip pullups	4 × 12, 10, 8, 6

Biceps

Ez-curl bar curls	4 × 12, 10, 8, 6
Alternate dumbbell curls	4 × 12, 10, 8, 6
Preacher curls	4 × 12, 10, 8, 6

Day 4: Shoulders and Traps
Shoulders

Shoulder presses	4 × 12, 10, 8, 6
Lateral raises	4 × 12, 10, 8, 6
Dumbbell presses	4 × 12, 10, 8, 6

Traps

Upright rows	4 × 12, 10, 8, 6

Day 5: Repeat Day 1

Day 6: Repeat Day 2

Day 7: Off

Day 8: Repeat Day 3

Chapter 21

KARL LIST–NATURAL PHYSIQUE ARTIST

BY LONNIE TEPER

Karl List doesn't seem like a chap who wants for much. After all, List and his wife, Jodi Friedman, not only share honors as two of the nation's finest natural bodybuilders, but they also share a wonderful life, both at home in their luxurious Marina del Rey, California, condo and at work at Gold's Gym, Venice, where they run a successful personal training business.

How could anything possibly be missing from List's life? Well, there's one small entity he wouldn't mind having at his disposal again every now and then. It's a dump—a small, smelly dump that's not any bigger than his current apartment and is filled with "250-pound morons trying to break everything in the room."

The dump that List recalls with such affection is the weight room at Slippery Rock State University in Pennsylvania, where he earned his degree in physical education a decade or so ago. It's "the greatest weight room I've ever worked out in," he said. "Everyone was hun-

gry—there was a lot of competitive energy in the gym. The first time I walked into the room, there were about 50 guys hanging out, and it was really hot. There was steam hanging in the air—it was great! Gold's in Venice is a great gym—I don't mean to put it down—but this place was just a different thing altogether. Probably more like the original Gold's was back in the early 1970s, when guys were just in there to crank beat-up weights, bend bars, and overtrain themselves into the ground."

That smelly little dump at Slippery Rock had an attitude about it. It's fitting that Karl should have a fondness for such a place because it was also an attitude—a bad one—that got him into weight training in the first place. Born in Portsmouth, Ohio, and raised along with his five siblings in various parts of Vermont, List was kicked off his high school basketball team at the age of 13 and headed straight for the place that housed the iron.

"That was probably the best thing that ever happened to me," he reflected, "because training with weights helped me correct my poor disposition—it gave me a physical outlet for my emotional problems."

List eventually matured, both physically and mentally, and became a two-sport star in football and track. In the latter he placed third in the decathlon in a Junior Superstars competition involving athletes from 14 states.

After graduating from high school in 1981, List labored at odd jobs for a couple of years, including pumping gas and working in a retirement home. Eventually, he retired from odd jobs and decided he wanted to attend a college with an odd name. Slippery Rock University, about 40 miles north of Pittsburgh, won the competition hands down.

He also decided it was time to make his bodybuilding debut. He placed third at the Mr. Vermont competition. "I was happy with the outcome, considering I dieted on milk and raisins," he said.

During his freshman year at Slippery Rock List won his first contest, the Western Pennsylvania. A year later he became president of the Slippery Rock Weightlifting Club, which had around 300 members. This gave him access to the dump from 3 A.M. to 5 P.M. every day.

The dump provided the pump for him to enter the Illinois Championships during his junior year. It was a good move, since Karl, who tipped the scales at 187 pounds on his 5′6″ frame, took the Light Heavyweight class. "I did the show because it was a week before the Nationals and I wanted to qualify," he said, "but I ended up deciding not to do the [Nationals]."

At that point in his career, his greatest strengths were "doing whatever I had to do to get in shape and the ability to pose what I have," he said. "I practiced a lot. I set up a mirror in my room in college, and every time I came into the room, I'd shut the door behind me and hit a couple of poses. That happened three, four times a day. The two poses I practiced the most were standing relaxed and front double-biceps."

Karl did make it to Atlantic City, New Jersey, for the Nationals in 1987, but not as a competitor. He went to lend support to his brother Arne, the youngest of the List clan, who

finished fifth in a Middleweight class that was won by Vince Comerford and his 21-inch guns.

"I don't know if I ever told my brother this," Karl said, "but I remember feeling Arne was getting ahead of me in bodybuilding, and it bothered me a bit. It provided Arne the fuel he needed, but all it gave me was insecurity because I was competitive with him. We weren't mean-spirited competitors—I love my brother. There was some envy on my part, no question. I remember driving down the street one day with my mom—this really put things into perspective—and she asked me if I'd rather be beaten by someone like my brother, a family member, or some stranger. The answer was easy."

After slipping through Slippery Rock, List spent almost a year as an assistant strength coach at the University of Maryland. From there he moved to Boston, where he finished second in the Light Heavyweight class at the '90 Gold's Classic. Arne had already moved to Southern California, and it was time to follow him to the mecca. In April 1991 Karl traded east for west in hopes of becoming one of the best.

"Arne, who had already been out here for a couple of years and was doing well personal training, told me he felt I had all the right tools to become a successful personal trainer in Venice, that I could make four times the amount of money here that I could make on the East Coast," he recalled. "A week later I was on a plane heading for California."

Arne was accurate in his assessment. Today Karl works about 60 hours a week, Jodi puts in another 25 or so, and they've become one of the most successful personal training teams in the area. Karl's client list is so large, in fact, that he works all the way up to contest day when he's competing.

While List's business ventures are doing splendidly, the same was not always said for his career on the posing dais. In 1992, when he was going through a divorce and just starting to date Jodi, he bombed at the USA, failing to make the cut as a Light Heavy. Jodi took top honors in the Middleweight division at that show.

"I put in about 16 years of training," he related. "This was my first national show, and I didn't make the cut. I wanted to go home when I found out, but Jodi said—this was the make-or-break part of our relationship—that if I left now, she wouldn't talk to me again. She just won the USA, and I bombed. The show was two days after my birthday, and I got trashed at the show. Then there was an earthquake the next day!"

Karl may not have made the cut, but he did make what was perhaps the most important decision of his bodybuilding career: He would do it the natural way or not do it at all. He waited until the '94 Los Angeles Bodybuilding Championships and won the Middleweight class. He then took another year and a half off before sweeping away the competition at the '95 Southern California Ironman Naturally contest, copping both the Light Heavyweight and Overall crowns.

Two weeks later List took the Middleweight division at the Huntington Beach

Championships before ending a successful 1995 with a third-place finish in the Light Heavies at the always-tough Tournament of Champions.

"I did drugs originally because I was seduced by the possibility of just how good I could be," he admitted. "I hadn't seen enough good natural bodybuilders, didn't believe they were out there. And I didn't believe in myself enough to think I could compete at a decent level and carry enough size to do well.

"[The decision to stop taking drugs] wasn't so much that I didn't think it was worth it. It wasn't what I was focusing on. If someone told me I could win the Mr. Olympia if I took everything I needed to do it, I would wrestle with it. And I don't honestly know what the answer to that would be. I was thinking about doing the USA next year but felt it would be a step backward, not forward, for me.

"I would love to do the Team Universe this summer, but Jodi and I have to go back to Vermont for a family reunion about a week and a half before the show [and] I haven't been home to see my family in two years," he continued. "I just can't take two weeks off from my work. If I leave for too long, I might lose clients. And Jodi also has the USA and the Nationals, so that's tying up a lot of time.

"That's just bodybuilding; we're also going to France for a week's vacation. At this stage I'm kicking around the idea of doing the Cal as a small Light Heavy, around 185 or so. I've always wanted to do that show."

As for other folks who might be wrestling with the dilemma he faced, Karl said, "I think one of the things you have to look at [is the emotional aspect]. When I got off, I had not suffered any side effects, physically, but there were things I went through emotionally. If you ask the bodybuilders who do steroids if they would compete if everybody else was clean, I think 90 percent of them would say no. I really believe that. Most of the bodybuilders who compete want to be big and freaky. And we know not too many of them, if any at all, can be big and freaky if they're not chemically enhanced. I'm not bashing anyone about it. It's an individual decision.

"But when I first got off of [steroids], I had an emotional battle within myself. I was walking back to the gym one day and I was telling myself that eventually you have to pay the piper. For some it's worse than others. For me, fortunately, [the side effects] were all emotional, wondering what it was that made me feel I had to be 250 pounds and squatting more weight than any human should squat. Why did I have to be stronger than anybody in the gym? I needed it because . . . I wasn't getting respect from people who were important to me.

"In our circle everybody gives immediate respect to a big guy when he walks into a room. He's instantly liked. What I had to deal with was my self-image, my feeling of self-worth without the need to be big. It helped being involved with Jodi. The first date I had with Jodi she told me she'd never done any drugs. Hey, I'm getting ready for the USA at that time and I'm thinking 'Yeah, and I just fell off the truck last night.' I mean, she's peeled! But I've been with her for four years, and [I know] there's not a drug in her body.

"You know, if we took bodybuilding back to an art instead of [focusing on] mass, sure, you'd have to have some muscle and be hard, but not to the degree where the result is an absolute freak that nobody outside of body-building is interested in looking at.

"I would say to the young kid coming up to be careful about what you read—because I wasn't. If I read someone was sissy squatting 1,000 pounds, my God I'd be in the gym the next day trying to sissy squat 1,000 pounds! And if your intention is to stay natural and you're having trouble with it, then read the natural magazines. Compare yourself to what you will be compared to. Compare yourself to a standard that's reasonable. Really do some soul searching. Ask yourself what is it inside of you that makes you so obsessed.

"I know some bodybuilders who compete on drugs who seem to have a very healthy mental attitude. They're not insecure, they have a career, they just really enjoy the body-building competition—and they want to compete at the highest possible level they can. To

those guys, if they understand the risk they're taking, [I say] go ahead and do what you need to do.

"I never felt good winning shows on drugs. I never felt victorious, like, 'Man, that was cool.' I was never good enough, never big enough. I never looked like the guy in the magazine. So, when I won my class at the L.A. without drugs, I felt that was a great win. I feel my natural physique is much prettier to look at; my shape is much nicer smaller. I hate to throw out names, but when Tim Belknap was a Light Heavy, he had a great build! But the heavier he got, the blockier he got. His physique got distorted, and that happens to a lot of guys who just want to get bigger and bigger.

"I'm interested in being as competitive as I can be. I don't know how good that is—I'm no Ronnie Coleman—but at 32 years old I have a better perspective as to what my limits are compared to a 22-year-old kid who really believes he's going to be the next Mr. Olympia. I can now realize that an admission of my genetic limitations does not mean I'm any less of a man."

KARL LIST'S PRECONTEST TRAINING

List emphasizes good nutritional habits, including proper supplementation. He believes that Sportpharma puts out some of the finest products available. "This company is high in integrity, their products are real clean, and they're high on developing new products," he said. "As far as I know, they were the first to produce vanadyl sulfate—they still make the best vanadyl sulfate.

"You must be patient when you're natural," he explained. "Don't try something for a week and then, if you don't think it's working, toss it. Give it eight weeks."

List says he takes in as much as 20 to 30 percent fat while on his precontest diet, but he keeps his carbohydrates to as low as 30 percent. "Your body needs fat to use fat," he pointed out. "If your body recognizes you're deficient in any nutrient, it's going to hold on to that nutrient, become very stubborn. What works for me is to diet down way ahead of contest time—be ready about four weeks out. That way I get about as lean as I'm going to get. Then I start to bring up my carbs."

As for his weight routine, List uses a four-day split in combination with a five-days-on/two-days-off schedule, as follows:

Monday: Day 1
Tuesday: Day 2
Wednesday: Day 3
Thursday: Day 4
Friday: Day 1
Saturday: Off
Sunday: Off
Monday: Cycle continues with Day 2

In 14 days he hits each bodypart "about 2¼ times," he said. Note that on leg day—Day 4—he squats once every two weeks, making it his first exercise of the day. He emphasizes complete, thorough warm-up sets on heavy squat days and goes up to 600 pounds.

Here's the breakdown—not including warm-ups.

Day 1: Chest and Shoulders*
Incline dumbbell presses 3 × 10–15

Flat-bench dumbbell presses	3 × 8–15
Cable crossovers	3 × 8–15
Dumbbell or machine front presses	3 × 8–15
Dumbbell or machine lateral raises	3 × 8–15
Wide-grip upright rows	3 × 8–15

*60 seconds between sets.

Day 2: Back, Rear Delts, and Traps

Front pulldowns or chins	3 × 8–15
Cable or machine seated rows	3 × 8–15
One-arm rows or Hammer pulldown machine	3 × 8–15
Hyperextensions	3 × 15
Machine vertical flyes	3 × 15
Lying lateral raises	3 × 15
Standing calf machine shrugs	3 × 10–20
Barbell or machine shrugs	3 × 15

Day 3: Biceps and Triceps

Seated dumbbell curls	3 × 8–15
Seated incline dumbbell curls	3 × 8–15
Preacher curls	3 × 8–15
Wide-grip pushdowns	3 × 10–15
Lying EZ-curl bar extensions or dumbbell extensions	3 × 10–15
Pushdowns	3 × 10–15

Day 4: Legs

Leg extensions*	3 × 10–15
Leg presses	3 × 10–15
Walking lunges	3 × 10–15
Seated leg curls	3 × 15
Lying leg curls	3 × 15
Stiff-legged deadlifts	3 × 15

*Or squats.

Karl works calves every Tuesday and Thursday. He does 9 sets, starting with donkey or standing calf raises, moving to reverse leg press raises and finishing with seated calf raises. As he said, "I'd rather sit on my ass at the end of my workout."

He works abs every Monday, Wednesday, and Friday, doing two main movements—crunches and reverse crunches, with some intercostal work thrown in occasionally. "I don't do a lot of machine work or high reps when I work my abs," List said. "I just do real intense, hard sets—3 sets of 20 reps."

Chapter 22

CHUNK TO HUNK

BY STEVE HOLMAN

Why do guys do it? What's the motivation? Why do they put themselves through the agony of lifting heavier and heavier weights day in and day out, year in and year out? Painful, burning reps. Buckets of salty sweat. For what? Sex appeal, plain and simple. Twenty-four-year-old drug-free bodybuilder Jonathan Lawson has no qualms about telling it like it is, insight he got directly from the mouths of babes:

"I had a lot of female friends in high school," said the Southern California bodybuilder. "As I started hanging out with them more and more, they began confiding in me, and I found out something many guys don't know: Women talk about guys' physical attributes just like guys talk about girls' bodies. Women may act like they don't notice, but believe me, they do."

Once this juicy tidbit came to his attention, Lawson decided that maybe it was time for him to go from dud to stud, from chunk to hunk, from cream puff to big and buff, from . . . well, you get the picture. He wasn't

playing any high school sports, so he joined a gym and began weight training with the hope of looking like Arnold—in a matter of months, of course.

While his workouts weren't all that consistent—when you have a lot of good-looking female friends who like to talk and cry on your shoulder, workouts can easily fall by the wayside—he did manage to add about 10 pounds of muscle, taking his skinny 150-pound body to a slightly less skinny 160-pound package. Unfortunately, that was far from his dream physique. Conan he wasn't.

After Lawson graduated from high school, he decided to dedicate himself to solid workouts and follow the bodybuilding champs' advice he read in the magazines. "I figured if I wanted to be big, I should look to the guys who are the biggest," he explained.

He started training like a man possessed, six to seven days per week, up to 20 sets per bodypart, and his physique transformed—but not in a good way. He did put on a pound or two of muscle in the beginning, but soon his

Jonathan Lawson.

gains sputtered from overtraining, he began eating everything in sight, and he got the "Dunlop" syndrome—that's where your belly "done lops" over your belt. While his insight into women's admiration of the male form conjured the notion of James Bond, his bodybuilding knowledge was more along the lines of Jethro Bodine from the *Beverly Hillbillies.*

"I was naive, to say the least. I didn't realize the incredible impact anabolic steroids have on building muscle—and that all the pros are on them," he recalled. "The training routines I followed were geared to work for bodybuilders on drugs, not natural bodybuilders like me. I overstressed my system and overate to compensate."

Once he was up to speed on this little fact, Jonathan adjusted his training, backed off on his calorie intake and actually progressed enough to enter a couple of contests. He never seemed to be big enough or cut enough to do very well, and after a few shows he thought that maybe this bodybuilding thing wasn't for

him—that, or perhaps he should try it with drugs.

Anabolic steroids were fairly easy to get around his gym, and guys were coming up to him all the time offering him a trial run with Mexican Dianabol or Anavar. Ah, the fringe benefits of living in Southern California. It was tempting, but Lawson wasn't going to revert to the naiveté of Jethro again. Instead, he decided to research the topic thoroughly before taking the plunge. Now in college, he did one of his first research papers on anabolic steroids, and what he found changed his outlook completely.

"The negative health consequences that can occur are endless," he said, "and taking drugs just wasn't worth the risk. Plus, because it's illegal, I knew guilt would eat me alive. I would feel as if I were cheating somehow."

So his dreams of building a great physique and winning a bodybuilding competition went up in a puff of smoke—or into the glute of some less-cautious bodybuilder via a syringe—or so he thought.

With towering disappointment but his integrity intact, Jonathan let his training slack

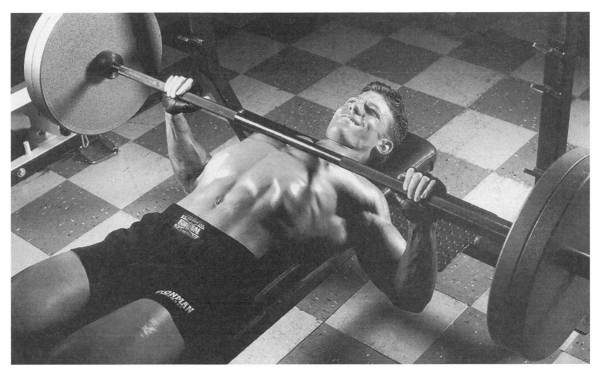

Bench press.

off. At age 21, with his bodyweight leveled off at a marshmallowy 190 pounds at 5'11", he began to refocus his priorities.

As chance would have it, he got a job in the product division of *Ironman* magazine around the time the 10-Week Size Surge program was being developed—at the end of 1994. At that point Lawson was still training, but he had no direction. Lawson didn't exactly look like a serious bodybuilder—more like a serious channel surfer. The Size Surge program made sense and motivated him to make a 2½-month commitment to double-check his potential. Was he really not cut out for bodybuilding? Ten weeks would tell the tale.

And how telling it was.

"To say I was shocked by the results I got from the 10-Week Size Surge program is putting it mildly. My muscle size took a radical leap: I added almost 20 pounds without an increase in bodyfat, according to caliper testing. My bodypart measurements and strength increases amazed me: arms, up 1¼ inches; thighs, up 1½ inches; waist, down 1 inch; bench, up from 200 × 10 to 290 × 6; squat, up from 205 × 8 to 335 × 7. And I did this with

Considering he was working full time as a customer service rep and going to night school for most of the year, Jonathan's victory was quite a remarkable accomplishment. What did he do differently? How did he make such dramatic progress from '96 to '97 and win his first Overall trophy? Here are a few things he learned that helped him get bigger and better, his seven natural laws, if you will:

1. **Maintain hard condition all year.** Lawson never lost sight of his abs, keeping his bodyweight at around 200 pounds for most of the year. Losing fat is a difficult process because you can lose muscle as well.
2. **Don't overtrain in the off-season.** Since his time was so limited, his off-season training was three days per week, working each bodypart only once every seven days.
3. **Don't overtrain during the precontest phase.** At 10 weeks away from the '97 Ironman Naturally, Jonathan's school semester ended and he ramped up his training but not as much as he had in

no steroids. Size Surge not only changed my physique, it changed my entire outlook on bodybuilding. I saw that I wasn't the hardgainer I thought I was."

After his successful Size Surge experience, which is chronicled in the book *20 Pounds of Muscle in 10 Weeks,* Jonathan shifted into a version of the fat-to-muscle program, added some cuts to his new mass and took home a couple of second-place trophies at drug-free contests, but first place continued to elude him. Bodybuilding is a continuous learning experience, and after tweaking his routine and diet to determine what works best for him, this past year he took first in his class as well as the Overall at the Southern California Ironman Naturally Novice and was in the best shape of his life.

’96. In ’96 he split his bodyparts over
three days with no days off—yes, he
trained seven days straight for about
15 weeks; for the ’97 show he split his
bodyparts over four workouts and took
Sundays off, and this precontest phase
only lasted 10 weeks. [See "Natural Law
Precontest Routine" on page 184 for his
winning program.]

4. **Use supersets.** He incorporated
   Compound and Isolation Aftershock
   supersets, which improved his muscle
   size and vascularity immensely.

5. **Don't overdo aerobics.** In ’96 he was
   running and walking the treadmill
   almost every day—and sometimes
   twice a day. In ’97 he walked the treadmill three to four times per week, relying more on small calorie cuts to get
   ripped. Reducing his aerobics decreased
   his cortisol surges, which resulted in
   much less catabolism than in ’96. His
   bodyweight actually dropped way down
   to a depleted 175 in ’96, with a lack of
   separation and hardness; a year later he

competed at somewhere between 180 and 190 pounds, ripped, with cross striations in his quads and triceps. He is looking to step on stage at close to 200 in solid condition in another two years—without chemical assistance, of course. Although he wants to get bigger, his primary concern is to maintain his proportions and symmetry and keep his Bob Paris–like lines.

6. **Use quality supplements.** Jonathan experimented with some new compounds Muscle-Linc's Cort-Bloc (phosphatidylserine, or PS).

7. **Try not to be too obsessive about the contest.** In '96 Jonathan was so totally focused, he burned out. In '97 he took the show less seriously, saw it as an opportunity to have fun and even let his diet slide a little every so often—but not too often.

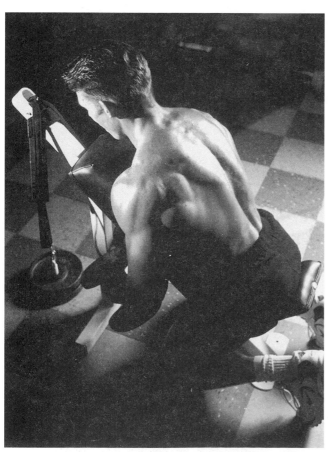

These forward-leaning dumbbell laterals produced a growth spurt in Jonathan's lateral delts.

All of this culminated in his victory and an *Ironman* cover, much to his delight—and relief.

"Being on the cover of *Ironman* is a dream come true and has inspired me to take my bodybuilding to the limit of my drug-free potential," he said, his voice rising with anticipation. "My growing collection of runner-up trophies was beginning to make me wonder if I had what it takes. It just goes to show you that persistence in bodybuilding, along with an open mind and learning what works for you, can pay off big."

And speaking of payoffs, how have the women responded to his new larger, more ripped physique? At the intermission after his contest win Lawson was answering questions. A good-looking woman made her way up to him and asked if she could give his beautiful body a hug. She proceeded to put her arms around him, testing his hardness by grabbing handfuls of his glute muscle for a good minute and a half. (I know this happened; I was there, staring with disbelief.) Why do guys work so damn hard in the gym? I think it's obvious.

NATURAL LAW PRECONTEST ROUTINE

Six days on, one day off

Day 1
Quads

Leg presses	3 × 8–10*
Aftershock superset	
Sissy squats	1 × 6–10
Leg extensions	1 × 6–8
Hack squats	2 × 6–10

Calves

Leg press calf raises	2 × 10–20*
Aftershock superset	
Donkey calf raises	2 × 10–12
Standing calf raises	2 × 10–12
Standing calf raises	1–2 × 30–40
Seated calf raises	2 × 10–12

Abs

Aftershock superset	
Ab bench crunch pulls	2 × 8–10
Incline kneeups	2 × 8–10

Day 2
Chest

Bench presses	3 × 8–10*
Aftershock superset	
Dumbbell flyes	1 × 6–8
Decline cable flyes	1 × 6–8
Cable flyes	2 × 8–10
Incline presses	2 × 8–10
Incline cable flyes	2 × 8–10

Lats

Front pulldowns	2 × 8–10*
Aftershock superset	
Dumbbell pullovers	1 × 6–8
Undergrip rows	1 × 6–8
Aftershock superset	
Pullover machine	1 × 6–8
Undergrip rows	1 × 6–8

Midback

Behind-the-neck pulldowns	2 × 8–10*
Supported T-bar rows	2 × 8–10
Shrugs	2 × 8–10

Rear delts/Midback

Bent-over laterals	2 × 8–10

Day 3
Hamstrings/Lower back

Stiff-legged deadlifts	2 × 8–10*
Leg curls	3 × 6–8*
Low-back machine	1 × 8–10*

Calves (light)

Donkey calf raises (light)	2 × 20*
One-leg calf raises	1 × 12–15
Standing calf raises (light)	2 × 20–40

Abs

Ab bench crunch pulls	1 × 8–10
Incline kneeups	2 × 8–10
Machine crunches	2 × 8–10

Neck

Manual-resistance at four positions	1 × 10–15

Day 4
Delts

Smith machine presses	2 × 8–10*
Forward-lean laterals	1–2 × 8–10
Aftershock superset	
One-arm incline laterals	2 × 6–9
One-arm laterals	2 × 6–9
Nautilus lateral machine	1 × 8–10

Triceps

Decline dumbbell extensions	2 × 8–10*
Aftershock superset	
Overhead extensions	1 × 6–9
Close-grip pushdowns	1 × 6–9
Aftershock superset	
Overhead extensions	1 × 6–9
Kickbacks	1 × 6–9
Bench dips	1 × 8–12

Biceps

Barbell curls	2 × 8–10*
Aftershock superset	
Incline curls	1 × 6–9
Close-grip curls	1 × 6–9
Aftershock superset	
Incline curls	1 × 6–9

| Preacher curls | 1 × 6–9 |
| Spider curls (on vertical side of preacher bench) | 1 × 8–10 |

Forearms
Superset

| Reverse wrist curls | 1 × 8–12 |
| Wrist curls | 1 × 8–12 |

Superset

| Reverse curls | 1 × 8–12 |
| Behind-the-back wrist curls | 1 × 8–12 |

*Do 1 or 2 warm-up sets with 50 to 70 percent of your work-set weight prior to your work sets.

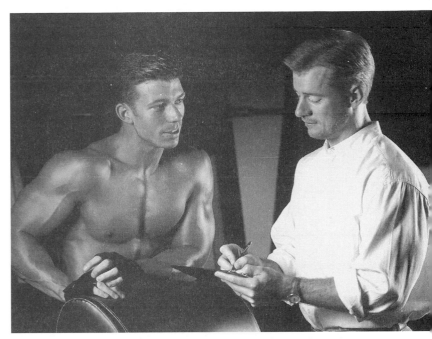

Jonathan and Steve Holman review the regimen that took Lawson to his first bodybuilding victory.

Chapter 23

SPICY BUT SIMPLE
SUSIE CURRY'S SMOKING WORKOUTS

BY RUTH SILVERMAN

CHAPTER PHOTOS BY J. M. MANION

The word *exotic* seems to follow Pro World champion Susie Curry around. There's her background, of course. The 24-year-old former gymnast from North Carolina with the spicy name and intriguing looks is an Army brat with a Vietnamese mother. She's lived all over the world—Germany, Korea, and New York. In the fitness arena she's caused quite a stir—the fastest-rising phenom to come along since Mia Finnegan. Curry is hot all right, and plenty exotic. When she gets into the gym, however, everything is strictly basic.

The second of three children, Susie started gymnastics at age 6, competing from age 10 through her years at North Carolina State, where she majored in biology. Although she was drawn to bodybuilding because she loves performing and quickly established herself as a prime contender in the routine round, she gets a lot of points for her physique as well. Her 5'2", 115-pound package is lean and elegant, and it was a major factor in the sweep of victories that took her to the top of the pro ranks

Susie Curry.

One-arm dumbbell row—start.

One-arm dumbbell row—finish.

in less than a year and to her first Fitness Olympia as a favorite to crack the top three— at the very least.

Her experience with weight training goes back to high school. "I did a lot [of it] for rehab," she explained, cheerfully ticking off a laundry list of gymnastics-related problems. "I had two knee surgeries, elbow surgery, fingers, you know—the works."

Nowadays the weights are part of an overall program that also includes cardiovascular work, routine practice, and training on the rowing machine, the latter in preparation for the only event in which she didn't excel at her Pro World victory in New York last May. At that show she didn't know what to expect. For the Olympia she is determined to be ready.

The same goes for her physique, for which her goal is "to put a little more lean muscle [on my upper body]. I've increased the weight and dropped the reps a little. Also, I tend to train real quickly, so I've slowed down a bit, and it's helped a lot."

Curry trains on a four-days-on/one-day-off schedule, using the following bodypart split:

Day 1: Chest and Biceps
Day 2: Legs
Day 3: Shoulders and Triceps
Day 4: Back

In gymnastics, where she competed at the national level, her favorite event was the balance beam. "It was the most challenging," she said. "I like doing floor routines because I like to perform, dance, tumble, but the balance beam is my favorite." In the gym, she said, "My favorite bodypart to train is back and my least favorite is legs."

As the above routine indicates, those are the bodyparts she usually trains by themselves. "I dread leg day, but I do it," she said. "I enjoy the results, so I train hard."

Curry works quads and hams together, "just to get it over with," and uses a routine built around those most basic exercises, squats and stiff-legged deadlifts. She does a maximum of three movements per muscle group and sticks with 12 to 15 reps "because I don't want my legs to get too big."

Hamstrings come first. "I'll warm up with leg curls and move on to stiff-legged deadlifts.

Undergrip pulldown—start.

Undergrip pulldown—finish.

I try not to fatigue my hamstrings too much before I move on to quads."

For thighs, she said, "I'll do squats, hack squats, leg extensions, and finish off with lunges."

Calf work she fits in whenever she has the time, often on back day, after she's put her body through a solid repertoire of basic pulling movements.

"I warm up with pullups and move on to lat pulldowns and seated rows and finish off with hyperextensions." She does 3 sets of 10 to 12 reps per exercise.

Curry never does more than 3 sets per exercise. "That's plenty of work," she said. "I feel it at the end."

Another thing she doesn't do is diet, something she admitted, somewhat abashed, only

Dumbbell lunges—left leg.

Dumbbell lunges—right leg.

Wide-grip pulldown—start.

Wide-grip pulldown—finish.

Leg curl—start.

Leg curl—finish.

after several probing queries from the reporter. "I eat pretty clean all year—and I've been blessed with a high metabolism." In fact, she did diet before the '97 Fitness International, and it proved to be a mistake. She came in too lean and scored the only non-first-place finish of her career, taking third behind Carol Semple-Marzetta and Monica Brant. For the Pro World she didn't diet—and that did the trick.

The self-described "shy-natured" Susie has "opened up a lot" since shooting to fitness stardom at the '96 NPC National Championship. At her first pro show, the International, she was "extremely nervous—going against these girls that I've seen on TV and in magazines—but I had a lot of fun, met a lot of people." As for her first Olympia, she was excited and looking forward to it, flattered that people were actually suggesting that she could win.

"Anybody could win it," said Curry, who moved to the Atlanta area last summer to open a gym with her sister and brother-in-law. "There's a lot of tough competition out there. It's just who's the best on that day. So you just go in hoping to do well."

With that attitude—and the following workouts—how can she lose?

Susie's Leg Day

Leg curls	3 × 12–15
Stiff-legged deadlifts	3 × 12–15
Squats	3 × 12–15
Hack squats	3 × 12–15
Leg extensions	3 × 12–15
Lunges	3 × 12–15

Back Day

Pullups	3 × 10–12
Lat pulldowns	3 × 10–12
Seated rows or one-arm dumbbell rows	3 × 10–12
Hyperextensions	3 × 10–12

Stiff-legged deadlift—start.

Stiff-legged deadlift—finish.

Shrug.

Chapter 24

MASS RIPPING TACTICS

BY DANIEL GWARTNEY, M.D.

In the quest for a championship physique most people start out training to get big; however, sheer size is not the pinnacle of bodybuilding. If it were, we'd see sumo wrestlers bodybuilding during their off-season. Obviously, the ideals of bodybuilding include a sculpted symmetrical physique that looks like something Michelangelo might have created—a hard, physical presence in an aesthetic presentation.

The key to building an ideal physique lies in finding a balance for the antithetical requirements of size and striations, density and definition, or however you want to describe the yin–yang relationship of gaining or keeping muscle while losing fat. To do that you need both a knowledge of the means available and an intuitive sense of how your body responds to every detail of your program. There is no pill, abdominizer, or Russian (or Bulgarian or any other Eastern bloc) secret that will get you huge and ripped at the same time. It takes time, experience, and a commitment to the details.

Not that there isn't value to many of the training approaches and supplements that are available, but too many people have false expectations that they can get in prize-winning shape by doing two hard weeks on some contraption or crash diet or using 10× dilution of "independently assayed" Mr. Olympia urinary extract. There is no free lunch.

I've been competing for 11 years, and bodybuilding has become a passion. At this stage of my career—and because of my involvement in the scientific end of things—I have the benefit of being recognized. With the recognition, however, comes the pressure of being a public personality under the gun to do well. On the other hand, I'm now able to afford the time and money involved in preparing for a competition without stressing, going broke, or having to sleep in my car (as opposed to the circumstances of my first few contests).

On November 20, 1998, I competed in the Musclemania competition in my best shape ever. At the age of 33 I brought my bodyfat down into the low single digits and actually had the easiest time of it. Granted, I have the experience gained from years of trial and error and better information than I did when I was starting out, and I have access to any supplement I choose. The success factor, however, was my having a realistic timetable and a scripted plan of action.

I train for a balance of symmetry, size, and definition, and I have always tried to walk on stage with a complete presentation. My years of competition have taught me a lot about what I don't want to look like. I've seen killer legs on guys who had no back and big upper bodies being held up by a pair of pencils. That isn't bodybuilding. Furthermore, I've seen razor-sharp, symmetrical competitors who looked as if they trained in a concentration camp. If you mistake your ribs for your obliques or serratus, or if the knee is the biggest part of your leg, you've got a problem.

You've also got a problem if your gut jiggles. I don't think male competitors should get on stage unless they're 6 percent bodyfat or less. That's what I shoot for.

What exactly is the ideal physique? Ask a dozen people and you'll get a dozen different answers. To my mind it starts with enough muscular development to signify strength. Bodyweight is a less-than-optimum measure of that, but it's convenient. I figure that at 5′8″ I should be at least 170 pounds. To adjust that goal to your own height, add 5 pounds for every inch taller than 5′8″ you are or subtract 5 pounds for every inch shorter. For example, if you're 5′10″, you should be at least 180 pounds. Beginning bodybuilders or teens may not yet have the muscle mass to hold that weight. Don't worry, as that's what time and training will provide.

Symmetry should be apparent. If you feel that you need to measure yourself, I recommend these goals: Your upper arms, neck, and calves should be equal in diameter. Your thighs should be close to your waist measurement.

Doctor Daniel Gwartney and his training partner, Chris Kelly.

Also, don't forget your back. The fact that you can't see it in the mirror doesn't excuse you from training it.

When it comes to tracking my bodyfat, I use skin-fold calipers and do not correct for age. The reason I don't is that the age difference basically refers to visceral, or organ, fat, while my only concern is subcutaneous fat, which is the fat that lies under the skin. I try to keep my skin folds at five millimeters or less, preferably two millimeters.

Now, before I get into the details of my program, I want to make it clear that I achieved my best-ever condition without using drugs. (If you want drug-related advice, ask your dealer, who probably doesn't even lift. There are plenty of clowns who have a Mr. Podunk title or competed in a national show eight years ago who can give you that kind of information.)

Miracles don't happen. You can't get ripped in 21 days. Heck, I wouldn't want that to be the case. If it were that easy, how would my effort stand out? How could I feel I'd accomplished anything?

I started my preparation for the November contest in late July. That gave me more than 16 weeks to get in contest shape. At my starting point, however, I was already looking as good as some guys I'd seen walk on stage, much to their embarrassment. I was 185 pounds and about 8 percent bodyfat. That gave me 16 weeks to lose 5 percent bodyfat. I wasn't going to worry about my weight as much as my size. In the past, whenever I dieted down to make a weight class, I ended up losing my look to meet the scale.

I usually start planning for a show about a year in advance, and when I commit to it, I realize that I'll be sacrificing a degree of my strength, regardless of my diet and supplements. When my bodyfat is between 8 and 10 percent, I can make tremendous gains; however, when I drop below that level, my strength drops along with my weight and bodyfat.

This chapter provides a rundown of the way I approach the various elements involved in getting ready for a bodybuilding competition.

DIET

The foremost factor in bodybuilding success is diet management. The most common mistake is to wait too long to begin dieting and cut calories too severely. I try to allow myself almost a month per 1 percent of bodyfat I'm trying to lose. That rate is based on a moderately low starting bodyfat, so if you're currently pulling your gut over your belt, plan for next year.

I take in about 2,800 calories daily on a maintenance diet. When I'm trying for serious gains, I may bump it up to 3,200; however, for the contest I dropped to 2,000. In the past I've dropped to 1,200 calories and lost a lot of muscle. Never again—diet is much more than counting calories. Even so, many people are pear-shaped on 2,000 calories a day. A person has to look at his or her body's tendencies.

I've become very obsessive about eating six meals a day and getting 30 to 40 grams of protein per meal. Meal-replacement powders are a convenient and relatively inexpensive way of working the extra protein into my daily schedule.

For the first eight weeks of my precontest diet I maintain a balanced macronutrient ratio—that is, one-third carbohydrates, one-third protein, and one-third fat. That simple change, along with a drop in calories, helped lower my bodyfat to 6 percent. As the fat loss was slowing down and my frustration was building, however, I knew I was not going to reach my goal of 3 percent.

Consequently, for the last eight to nine weeks of the diet I dropped my carbohydrates while maintaining my calories at 2,000 per day. Obviously, I was replacing the carb calories with protein and fat. As I am very carb sensitive, that strategy worked very well for me, but it may not work as well for everyone. By the time I reached the four-week mark on the revised plan, my bodyfat had decreased to 4 percent.

A funny thing about bodybuilding is that you can do all the right things but peak too early. To avoid that, I purposely increased my calories but maintained the carb restriction, keeping my intake at less than 60 grams a day. I haven't figured out the reason, but it made me very lean and vascular. I had workouts in which every vein from my fingertips to my toes was showing. I didn't expect that, since I was basically going through a prolonged carb depletion. My diet was successful, leaning me out while allowing me to maintain my strength and size. I have to admit, this is the first time I ever hit it dead on.

The one mistake I made was in carbing up for the show. I had a fairly long photo shoot on the day before the contest, during which I carbed up slowly using a 40/30/30 meal bar. I know I have that tendency to hold water if I have too many carbs, so, in retrospect, I was probably too strict about my water intake during the shoot, which may have flattened me the next day. On show day I diuresed—that is, flushed all my water—and didn't eat until the weigh-ins. That strategy was too successful, as I dropped a weight class and ended up being two to four inches taller than the rest of the competitors, which may have hurt me in the comparisons.

Decline dumbbell press.

To carb up, I ate papaya coated with honey throughout the day, along with a high-sugar meal-replacement bar. Don't ask me why; it just sounded good. Unfortunately, by the time the show started, I was feeling like a balloon at the Macy's Thanksgiving parade. The papaya had so much fiber that my happy little bowel bacteria were bubbling away in an orgy of hydrogen gas. Fortunately, my suffering wasn't too apparent on the outside, although I did notice water creeping under my skin and was considering a quick trip to the sauna. The sauna would have been a mistake, however, as the sweat would have caused the tanning dye to run. My girlfriend and training partner, Chris Kelly, was excellent about providing me with support, encouragement, and red wine.

TRAINING

During the year I returned to heavy training and had a goal of benching five plates, or 495 pounds. Heavy training always adds size to my

Rope-grip pulldown.

muscles. The year before I'd focused on getting killer striations with high-intensity, high-rep training, which worked, but it left out the hypertrophy effect of overloading the muscle.

Every year I try to learn more about the way my body responds. This time I stayed with the heavy free-weight training, and I'm glad I did. I came on stage just as lean as I had been the previous year but with a much fuller appearance. Chris and I train nearly every day, regardless of whether one of us is getting ready to compete. We use an eight-day split and work only one bodypart per day, but we work it completely. We hold nothing back for a second bodypart or another workout for the same bodypart in three or four days. That enables us to perform more sets and stay heavy throughout the workout once the muscle is warmed up.

Our split treats all bodyparts equally. I realize that certain muscle groups, usually the smaller ones, recover more quickly; however, the groups that need to be worked more frequently typically contribute to the movements of the larger muscles. Examples would be the triceps' involvement in pressing exercises for the chest, or the calves' involvement in both hamstring and quad movements.

I've found that my approach to training is different from most people's. Thanks to my medical background, I understand the functions and structure of the muscles and joints. That, combined with my experience, has led me to train using different angles, rotations, and contraction patterns. I've received a lot of positive feedback from people I've shared the information with and seen quite a few succeed using my methods. The details are beyond the scope of this chapter, but I will give you an idea of my overall approach to training.

I do not stretch before lifting. I use my warm-up sets to stretch the muscles by working them through the whole range of motion. That makes a lot more sense than grabbing a limb and stressing it across a joint. Unless you stretch for at least 30 minutes, there's really no point. I don't see what 15 to 30 seconds of tugging accomplishes. That's like doing 50 crunches on an abdominizing machine and expecting to have abs.

I'm an old-fashioned lifter. I stick with increasing weights on a modified-pyramid scheme. I warm up or do a light set, then a moderate set. I do 2 or 3 heavy sets and then 1 light set using strict form to force myself to burnout. The rest between sets is about the time it takes to help Chris do her set and get focused. If I find that I'm breathing heavily, I slow down until my respiratory rate is close to normal.

Even though I train heavy, I use a fairly high rep range, and it helps me maintain the definition I spent significant time acquiring. Sometimes this means poor Chris gets a workout spotting me.

I always try to work through a full range of movement. I see a lot of people do exercises like triceps extensions with so much hip, back, and shoulder motion that they hardly have to bend their elbows. I also try to move slowly at the beginning of the motion so I won't be finishing it with momentum. Think about the guys you see doing leg extensions with the pad off their legs after liftoff. How much work are they actually doing?

There's a popular notion that you should work a set to failure. On certain lifts I try to take each rep to failure. The stimulus for muscle growth and development—as well as connective tissue growth and repair—is muscle tension. Typically, people achieve maximal muscle tension by overloading the muscle with near-maximum weight. That's effective, but it only works at the beginning of the movement. You can't achieve maximal muscle tension at the completion of a rep, particularly if you're performing swinging, momentum-laden movements. That's one of the reasons many people can't complete a lot of reps at near-maximal loads. They never develop their strength along the entire curve.

The concept of completing each rep to failure doesn't apply to all exercises. For example, it would be hard to use in power movements, but it's perfect for the isolation exercises.

Our workouts take about 45 minutes. Many great workouts have been completed in even less time than that. So even though I'm in the gym seven days a week, I put in less than six hours a week training. Some weeks it's less than five hours. As I am a father and have work obligations, time is a critical factor for me.

SUPPLEMENTATION

Don't hide your wallets. This is not the hidden sales-pitch portion of the discussion. Unless you train seriously, and I mean *seriously*, the supplementation program outlined here is probably much more than you need. Also, although many of the supplements I use are "comped" to me, I do purchase some products. I also remember the days of dropping $400 at GNC's gold card sale or buying the crap brands because I could not afford the quality stuff. Even now when I'm shopping for supplements I look for the best deal on quality products.

Here are a few points that may save you from disappointment or from falling prey to some of the sharks in the industry. First of all, remember that supplements are meant to be supplemental. They aren't magic powders, potions, or pills. They don't go to the gym for you or correct your bad habits. If you don't control your diet and are not disciplined about your training and lifestyle, don't buy supplements! You'll just have a nonproductive cycle of whatever you take and ruin the reputation of the decent products out there.

Keep a log of your training and diet for one month before using any product, then continue that log while using the product for at least two months. If you get no effect—and you were looking for the right effect for that supplement—call the company and, if necessary, get your money back. The manufacturer may educate you about something you were missing or you may be one of the few true nonresponders. (They do exist, even with the best supplements, but if a product is truly effective, there can't be that many genetic variants in the world.)

My supplement program was designed to maximize fat loss while maintaining the muscle mass I'd built. I have enough self-confidence to accept that, despite my having the best supple-

Daniel Gwartney, M.D.

ments, diet, training, and support, I would still lose some muscle mass. Without pharmaceutical assistance, avoiding muscle loss would take genetic gifts that I don't have.

I planned my supplementation program in tandem with my diet plan. During the first eight weeks I took adequate supplements to support a moderate amount of progress. The second half of my program involved a more elaborate supplementation scheme.

For the first eight weeks I used three different types of supplements: proanabolic; prolipolytic, or fat-burning; and repair-and-support. Some of the products I took fell into more than one category. The proanabolic supplements for maintaining muscle mass included effervescent creatine with phosphate, insulin mimickers (lipoic acid, vanadium, selenium, and taurine), and androgen precursors. I am hesitant to mention the androgen precursors, as I don't endorse their use, but you deserve my honesty.

The prolipolytic supplements for accelerating fat burning included guggulsterones (the active ingredient in Commiphora mukul, now

Greg Blount.

included in Muscle-Linc's Thyro Stak), and Adipokinetics, which includes a modification of the ephedrine-and-caffeine stack with the addition of yohimbine. I would caution everyone to consult with his or her physician before using an ephedrine-and-caffeine-type combination.

The last class of supplement I took, repair-and-support, included antioxidants and glutamine.

The final eight weeks or so of my contest prep were really intense, and the physical and mental stresses began to mount. Knowing that, I increased my use of some of the previously mentioned supplements, kept other dosages the same, and added new ones. Since I dropped my carbs way down for the last half of my preparation, which would lead to a loss of the natural release of insulin and its anabolic/anticatabolic effects, I had to maximize my proanabolic supplementation. As the effervescent creatine contained 20 grams of carb, I stayed at one serving daily, first thing in the morning. I increased all of my insulin mimickers, taking some with each

meal. Finally, I increased my androgen precursors to twice a day, taking them first thing in the morning and last thing at night. That led to some nipple tenderness, which, fortunately, went away after I stopped using the products.

Knowing that my diet manipulations should force my body to break down my long-term energy stores—which is a nice way of saying fat—I didn't increase my use of Adipokinetics. Since I was dropping my carbs so low, a condition that decreases thyroid hormone activity, however, I increased my use of guggulsterones by one dose per day.

I also began to use three new supplements. I know HMB does not have an effect you can feel, but the science on it is too good to ignore. I have never felt overtrained on HMB, and I was certainly setting myself up for overtraining, muscle breakdown, or catching a cold due to a depressed immune state. So with a dash of logic and a pinch of faith I added HMB to my supplement regimen.

To further my protection from the evils of excess cortisol, I also began to use Cort-Bloc, a source of phosphatidylserine. Once again, the science is impossible to ignore. In addition, I figured that if I was going to do the show, I was not going to hold anything back.

The last supplement I added was GH Stak. I had once created a growth hormone releaser and knew the area cold. I admit that my product is not as potent as GH Stak, but it was never meant to be, as it was designed to be cheap and cost effective. My product was supposed to be taken two to three times a day—at twice the recommended dose—but the marketer made the margin so high that it was cost prohibitive to take that much. That's too bad, since Chris and I both saw good results. In any event using the GH Stak was a good move for me. For the first time in years my tendinitis went away. Also, my condition continued to harden, and I had no problem with energy or feeling overtrained. Unfortunately, I'm not any taller.

The bad news about my supplement program is that I can't say definitely whether one product worked or one didn't, since I was using so many. All I can say is that I looked my best.

Whatever supplements you choose, there's one vital element that cannot be neglected—water. Hydration is so important that every issue of every bodybuilding magazine should include an article on water. I drank so much that I thought I was going to grow gills. I was drinking more than two gallons a day, making trips to the bathroom every 20 minutes at certain parts of the day and getting up three or more times a night. I know some jobs don't lend themselves to hourly potty breaks, so you'll have to figure out how to accommodate your schedule. A rule of thumb I use to determine how much water to drink is that my urine should be colorless. If it's yellow or darker, then I'm dehydrated.

POSING

I do no cardio. I believe it was designed by some guy who was tired of getting sand kicked in his face. So, rather than hit the gym, he convinced all the big guys to lose every shred

of muscle they had by doing cardio. Seriously, you should do cardiovascular training for health reasons, not to get cut. Otherwise, you'll sacrifice a lot of muscle.

If you need to burn calories, try one of two things. Either sit in a tub of cold water up to your chin or practice your posing. Anyone who thinks that posing isn't hard work has never done it. Practicing posing is one of the best things you can do to harden up, and it will condition you for the stage. I start posing eight weeks out, building up from twice a week to four times a week. I also try to hold my poses longer and have someone critique

them as show day draws near. If you have a mirror, use it. Don't neglect your back, hams, and calves just because you don't have eyes in the back of your head.

LIFESTYLE

Even when I'm training hard for a show, I have certain outside obligations. I have a beautiful six-year-old daughter, and I spend time with her. I see most of my extended family regularly and have a relationship with Chris. Outside of that, my training and work obligations are all I have. I cut out all social distractions and try to minimize my obligations while I prepare for a show. It's tough, but I've made my choice. (If bodybuilding were all fun, wouldn't everyone have been Mr. Big Fish in a Small Pond?)

One of my few regrets about bodybuilding is the demands it places on my family. I can handle being antisocial for a short time, but there's no excuse for behaving that way with my family. Also, it takes me out of leisure activities—like dining out, having friends over for pay-per-view boxing with nachos, enjoying a wine the name of which I can't pronounce or a

beer the name of which I can. That means my daughter is held to the same Spartan lifestyle as I am, and so is Chris. I thank God my family knows how important this is to me and that Chris can participate. There have been days when the only civil words we spoke were during our training. There have been many, many more days when Chris was the only person who believed in what I was doing. If you have a spouse and/or children, include them in your plans. They are stuck in the house with a bodybuilder. I'd bet that, given a choice, a lot of them would rather have roaches.

This year was not so bad, and we think that's partially because I didn't use ephedrine. When I did use it, I had terrible food cravings, and I was very irritable. I used the Adipokinetics, but the norephedrine did not cause the same problems.

The least tolerable part of the whole process for me was tanning. I don't know why, but it tires me out. I think it's a dehydration thing. Using a tanning bed must not be any worse for you than, say, tobacco or alcohol, since the government doesn't restrict it. I don't recommend using a tanning bed but I have to admit I did use one.

MISCELLANEOUS

There are a lot of voodoo practices people use. Everyone has his or her own personal secrets. Here are some of mine.

- Use Pam or some other brand of cooking oil spray. It goes on evenly and lightly and won't streak your tanning dye. Don't be the goof who uses garlic- or butter-flavored spray. It stinks.
- Tanning dyes don't work if you don't have a tan. You'll look like a sick Smurf or the carrot from the third-grade "Peter Cottontail" play. I tan to get a good base, then apply a product called Sun by Giessee twice a day for four days starting a week out. Then I apply a thick coat of Dream Tan daily.
- Don't eat a lot of carbs at once when you're carbing up—and no fruits or vegetables. They're good at any other time but will give you gas when you're carbing up. I use a meal-replacement bar that contains 30 grams of simple sugars.
- Know how to shave, especially your bikini line. It is no fun judging someone who has a herpes-looking rash around the groin.
- Have a backup tape for your music and have them both cued. Music delays kill a show.
- Tell your friends and family to cheer loudly. If it's silent when you hit your poses, people may as well be telling you to get off the stage.
- Don't tan, use the sauna, or fly on the day of the show or the day before. It will cause your skin to hold water.
- Don't enter a drug-free show if you aren't drug-free. It wastes your money and ruins your reputation.

Chapter 25

THE FAT-BURNING WORKOUT

BY MICHAEL GÜNDILL

You may wonder why everything seems to go wrong when you start a low-calorie diet. Within a few days your strong motivation vanishes, and you feel increasingly less energetic. Your training weights start decreasing along with your training intensity, and what you see in the mirror is even worse: You're shrinking. Your goal was to lose fat, but you just look smaller, not leaner. In fact, you look flabby, and your muscles are flattening rapidly.

You blame your diet, and you swear to try a better one next time, but—surprise!—there may be nothing wrong with your diet or your supplementation. The problem is probably your training.

WHEN SUPPLY DOESN'T MEET DEMAND

Your fat stores hold lots of usable calories— there's far more fuel than you might imagine—and diets are designed to get your body to use part of that huge energy reserve.

Paradoxically, after a few days of dieting, you feel as if the demand for energy is not being met, as if your body has developed some kind of resistance to the fat energy. It seems to be the wrong fuel, as if you were putting kerosene into your car. It's a great source of energy for flying airplanes, but somehow your car can't use it.

Unlike your car, however, your body is supposed to adapt to almost any source of energy available. There are only three sources of energy your body can store: carbohydrates, fats, and proteins. It's very rare that it uses only one of them. Rather, it usually oxidizes a combination of the three. As a bodybuilder you eat plenty of carbs and proteins in the off-season. When you go on a diet, you start cutting down the calories coming from fat. The carbs are the next to go, but protein intake is rarely affected. The big leap of faith is that you assume that your body is good at shifting from one energy source to another. In the off-season it's used to getting plenty of carbs. Suddenly, it's expected to forget about carbs and immediately turn into an efficient fat-burning machine. That's a very wrong assumption. It's not that your body can't accomplish the metabolic shift; it's just that the process is not as simple as it seems.

As you start your diet and cut your carb intake, your body is left with basically two sources of energy: the fat found in the adipose tissue—which you want to burn—and the amino acids found in your muscles, which you want to spare. Of course, there will be some carbohydrates left but certainly not enough to meet the caloric demand.

Your body will go for the energy source it knows how to use best: proteins. Proteins are relatively easy to use, and your body is full of them thanks to your hypertrophied muscle

mass. This is the beginning of a long catabolic phase. Your body will use your muscles for energy and so will spare your adipose tissue.

Why aren't bodybuilders good at using fat as energy? The answer is easy. Without realizing it, they do things that prevent their bodies from burning fat.

TRAINING IS EVERYTHING

As mentioned above, training is the most important factor, the one that will make your diet a success or failure. Of course, the diet itself counts, but the average bodybuilder knows approximately how to design a low-calorie diet. As you can imagine, your muscles,

Patrick Lynn.

based on their size, are a major source of energy consumption. That's not just true during a workout but also throughout the day. When you're on a low-calorie diet, your muscles get increasingly weaker, which indicates that something's really wrong. Your body doesn't know how to use its own fat, and because you're restricting carbs, you're forcing it to use the only energy source available—your muscles. That's the reason you shrink and don't look leaner as you diet.

You train your muscles to get bigger and stronger, not to use fat as energy. As with most things in life, however, you have to practice to be good at something. So, if you want your muscles to use fat as energy, you have to train them to do it. Chances are, if you follow conventional bodybuilding workouts, you're teaching your muscles to avoid using fat for energy. Most bodybuilders train in ways that prevent them from being good at burning fat.

You may argue that you ride a stationary bike regularly, which is a good way to force your muscles to burn fat as energy. That's not true. Riding a bike only teaches a small portion of your legs to use fat as energy. It does nothing for the rest of your muscles.

WHAT MAKES A FIBER GOOD AT BURNING FAT?

There two kinds of muscle fibers inside every muscle, type 1 and type 2. The type 2 fibers are the easiest to hypertrophy, which makes them your primary target in bodybuilding. They're good at using carbs, but they aren't so good at burning fat. The type 1 fibers, on the other hand, are best at oxidizing fat, but they're frequently neglected by bodybuilders, as they're less likely to hypertrophy. Even if you somehow stimulate those fibers, you usually don't train them to burn fat. Training for mass is fine as long as all you want are big muscles fast, no matter what the cost is in terms of excess bodyfat. If you care about your appearance, however, it's a major mistake to ignore those fibers.

Think of it as a competition between the muscle fibers. By training only with heavy weights and low reps to cause the type 2 fibers to hypertrophy, you cause some of the type 1 fibers to be transformed into type 2.[1] As a result, the number of type 1 fibers is reduced, and over the long term bodybuilders' muscles tend to become predominantly composed of hypertrophied type 2 fibers. While the type 1 fibers may sometimes be called on by mistake, they're rarely stimulated properly. The situation is even worse in drug users, as many drugs accelerate the shift from type 1 to type 2 fibers.

When you go on a low-calorie diet, some of the fat inside your adipose tissue is released and passes into the blood. As that happens, the fat is supposed to be drawn to the muscles for oxidation as energy. If you use the supplements I recommend in this chapter, you should have more than enough fat circulating in your blood. The amount of fat your muscle can attract represents the first bottleneck.

The uptake of fat by muscles is made possible by an enzyme called lipoprotein lipase.[2] Type 1 fibers contain plenty of lipoprotein lipase, while type 2 fibers do not. As a result, your muscles aren't efficient at attracting the circulating fats.

Only a limited amount of fat will make it inside your muscles, where it should reach the mitochondria for oxidation. There are plenty of membranes to cross.[3] The old idea called the flip-flop theory stated that fatty acids were freely and passively transported inside the muscle fibers.[4] This works in a test tube on synthetic membranes, but, unfortunately, it's a different story in your muscles.[5] Once they're inside the muscles, the fatty acids have to be transported by carriers, so the amount of fat that can reach the mitochondria is limited by the number of carriers. Type 2 muscle fibers don't have many fat carriers inside them. Type 1 fibers, on the other hand, have plenty. What's more, whenever you train type 1 fibers properly, the number of carriers increases and each carrier becomes more efficient at transporting fat.[6]

It's crucial that you understand that the adaptation is localized to the properly trained

Lateral raises.   Joe DeAngelis.

Oxidation of fatty acids

The purpose of fatty acid oxidation inside the muscle is to manufacture ATP for muscle contractions, a transformation that takes place in the mitochondria. Type 2 fibers mostly use carbohydrates as energy and are not richly endowed with mitochondria. That situation is compounded by the fact that bodybuilders often use carb drinks before or during workouts in the off-season. When you elevate the level of carbohydrates in your blood, your muscles don't have to rely on fat for energy. That further represses the pathways that permit muscles to burn fat.

This is not to say that it's bad to drink carbs during a workout—in fact, it's a smart strategy for packing on muscle mass. By making carbohydrates easily available during workouts, however, you train your muscles to be good at using carbs for energy while detraining them at burning fat. Based on that fact, you cannot expect your muscles to be good at using fat just because you decided to

muscles. An example cited above applies here: When you ride a bike, you train a small part of your leg muscles to be good at using fat; but the exercise does nothing for the muscles in the rest of your body.

That's the first limiting step for bodybuilders: Very little fat reaches your muscle, and once it's inside the type 2 fibers, the rate of transport of fatty acids is very slow. In other words, hypertrophied type 2 fibers make it hard for fat energy to become available. That will be true no matter how you train. Fats are not a great source of energy for intense contractions. As a result, your muscles become proficient at using carbohydrates while they forget about using fat. Although that's not too troublesome in the off-season, it will cause major problems when you're on a diet. The point is, you should train the type 1 fibers in all your muscles to counteract the natural bodybuilding-induced resistance to fat transport.

Weighted chins.   Joe DeAngelis.

go on a diet. In addition, carb drinks elevate your insulin level, which impairs fat oxidation as well. When insulin is elevated, the fat oxidation pathways are blunted. Again, that doesn't make insulin bad. In fact, a slight elevation of insulin is probably a prerequisite for muscle growth.

The key point here is that building muscles and losing fat are two completely different situations. Being good at building muscle mass doesn't mean you can easily get lean; likewise, lean people have trouble putting on muscle. The biochemical pathways are different and you must train each of them separately so they become more efficient.

Two fat storage areas

As a bodybuilder you're concerned with two main sites of fat storage. The most obvious is between your muscles and your skin. It's called subcutaneous fat, and in normal people around 80 percent of the fat is stored there. That's the fat that makes you look bad in the mirror. The second type of fat is intramuscular fat that's stored in the form of muscle triglycerides. With the subcutaneous fat representing the main depot of adipose tissue, only a small amount is left to go inside the muscle. The intramuscular fat is desirable, however, as it makes your muscles look bigger. For a given bodyfat percentage, the higher the level of intramuscular triglycerides, the less subcutaneous fat you'll have.

The principle is similar to what happens with carbs. What's the point of carbing up? To get as much carbohydrate inside your muscles as possible to blow them up. Strictly speaking, your muscle mass isn't any greater after you carb up. Your muscles are just full of glycogen. It's exactly the same with fat. Filling up the muscles with fat makes them look bigger.

Muscle fat has gotten a bad rap because intramuscular triglycerides are usually high in cases of obesity as well as some forms of diabetes.[7] For years scientists couldn't determine the reason it was unhealthy for such patients to have a high fat content in their muscles when it was so positive for athletes to have that fat. Only now are the reasons for the dis-

Jim Shiebler.

crepancy becoming clear. It seems that muscles have several ways of holding fat. One is an unhealthy way, in which triglycerides seem to invade the whole muscle, and another is a healthy way, in which muscle fat is found to be extremely close to the mitochondria. Such fat provides muscles with quick energy to sustain prolonged muscle contractions while avoiding all the transport problems.

For bodybuilding purposes it would be great to store all your fat inside the muscle instead of in the subcutaneous areas. You'd never look fat, and your muscles would seem huge. While that isn't possible, it is possible to get a lot of fat to relocate inside the muscles rather than around the muscles, where it makes you look smooth. Your best allies in reaching that goal are the type 1 fibers, which have a high capacity for storing intramuscular triglycerides. The type 2 fibers, on the other hand, have a very limited capacity for holding fat. Training mostly type 2 fibers reorients the fat toward the subcutaneous depots rather than inside the muscles, while specifically training the type 1 fibers means that less fat is stored in the subcutaneous areas than what usually happens in bodybuilders. The latter is an easy, drug-free way to look bigger and leaner.

There's an additional benefit of storing the fat inside the muscle instead of below the skin. The more fat found inside the muscle, the higher the basal metabolic rate and so the greater the energy expenditure. Scientists have discovered this relationship to be true but are as yet unable to explain it fully. The most likely explanation might be that subcutaneous fat prevents your body heat from radiating out. It provides efficient insulation, making it easier for your body to maintain its temperature. If you have less subcutaneous fat, however, more heat radiates out of your body and your body burns more energy trying to maintain body temperature.

THE FAT-BURNING WORKOUT

Losing weight isn't easy. It's even harder if you're trying to lose only fat while holding on to muscle. Contrary to the typical measures taken by bodybuilders, your first goal should be to recover the pathways that allow your muscles to burn fat—and make them very good at it. Obviously, that's not going to happen in a few days, so you don't want to start worrying about it a week before you start dieting. Besides, by that time it's too late. Just as you train your muscles all year long to get bigger, you have to train them all year long to burn fat. Not only will things be easier while you're on a diet, but it will also help you look bigger and leaner during the off-season.

Energy provided by fat isn't the proper source for intense muscle contractions. Your main goal here is to train your muscles to be good at oxidizing fat while they're at rest. Muscle mass, because of its volume, should be a major location for fat oxidation. Otherwise, you'll be good at storing excess bodyfat and very bad at losing it. That's the reason obesity

is related to impaired fat oxidation by muscles. When your muscles become good at burning fat, they use up triglycerides as energy throughout the day. Both muscle proteins and muscle glycogen are spared, and fuel is more rapidly available during your workouts to sustain intense muscle contractions. Fat energy will only supplement glycogen as energy during a workout. The result will be a more intense workout despite the diet and more fat oxidation during the rest of the day.

Off-season: Hit the type 1 fibers

While you need fully efficient type 1 fibers during a diet, they'll also help fat relocate into the muscles during the off-season. In addition, type 1 fibers can be made to hypertrophy, although to a lesser degree than type 2 fibers. Your off-season training goals for the type 1 fibers are the following:

1. Prevent atrophy of the pathways allowing fat oxidation.
2. Make them more efficient.
3. Relocate fat storage from subcutaneous adipose tissue to intramuscular fat.
4. Cause type 1 muscle fibers to hypertrophy.
5. Train the muscles to be good at performing high reps.

It's possible to accomplish those goals by performing a few high-rep sets at the end of your workouts. Once you're done with a bodypart, add 2 sets of 50 reps for that muscle group. Use one or two single-joint, or isolation, exercises. Also, do one 100-rep set for a bodypart you aren't training directly that day, as follows:

After back, do a set of 100 reps for shoulders.
After chest, do a set of 100 reps for calves.
After hamstrings, do a set of 100 reps for quads.
After quads, do a set of 100 reps for hamstrings.
After shoulders, do a set of 100 reps for back.

Cable crossovers.   Henrik Thamasian.

After biceps, do a set of 100 reps for
triceps.
After calves, do a set of 100 reps for
chest.

Why 100 reps? It's a symbolic figure rather
than a magic number. Fewer than 100 is probably too little to really stimulate the fat pathways in fresh muscles. More than 100 seems
to take forever and forces you to drop the
poundage even more.

Some people may argue that doing so
many reps induces muscle loss. That's not
true. The comment usually comes from people
whose muscles aren't efficient at performing
high repetitions and using fat as energy. Once
you start training your muscles regularly with
high reps, you'll discover that they can handle
a significant amount of weight. Furthermore,
by stimulating blood flow, you'll enable your

Chris Faildo.

muscles to recover faster not only between
workouts but also between heavy sets.

To avoid performing too many sets, you
might want to cut down on the number of
standard low-rep sets you do. A good rule of
thumb is to maintain your previous workout
length when you include the high-rep sets. The
high-rep training should take less than 10
minutes. See how many conventional sets
you do in 10 minutes. Then you'll know how
many sets you should eliminate—usually 2 or
3 at most.

The transition period

This period is most important, as it determines the success of your diet. The goal is to
train the fat-burning pathways to be fully
efficient before you start the diet. That's a key
point. You want to start your diet knowing
that those pathways are maximally developed
and ready to replace the pathways that enable
carb combustion. You don't want to have to
develop them during the diet. Ideally, you
should start the transition 30 days before the
actual diet. If you're in a hurry, take at least
15 days. The off-season work wasn't meant to
develop the fat-burning pathways maximally
but to prepare you for the fat burning to
come.

The purpose of this transition period is to
train the type 1 fibers more frequently with
more reps. You train your entire body over two
days, followed by a rest day. You train some
bodyparts with heavy weights to retain muscle
mass; you don't want to eliminate the overload
that increased your mass, but you reduce it to
a bare minimum to work on another aspect of
the muscles.

For this period you train your muscles
in a modified superset fashion. For example,
when you do chest and back, perform 1 set for
chest, rest, and then do a set for back, etc.

For your lower body superset quads with
hamstrings and calves with abs. The modified
superset lets you accelerate the pace of your
workout while enhancing recuperation. It's
based on the fact that muscle recovery is faster
when you stimulate the antagonist muscle.
Training a bodypart forces the antagonist

muscles to relax. When you do straight sets, the trained muscles remain slightly contracted, which delays full recovery.

Note that when you do light training, you use single-joint movements. When you do heavy training, choose compound movements and finish with a single-joint exercise for the big muscle groups.

As you get used to this program, you can add aerobics on the rest day. Rowing is best, as it stimulates both the upper and the lower body; but don't do too much, as aerobic training and big muscles don't mix. Too much aerobic exercise will impair muscle growth.

This type of training is not necessarily restricted to the period preceding a diet. If you tend to accumulate fat even though you're not eating excessively, this training can help. Remember that many obese people become fat because they're unable to oxidize fat, an impairment that's primarily located in muscles. Many studies have demonstrated that you're less likely to accumulate bodyfat when you have a greater capacity for fatty acid oxidation.

Fat-burning supplementation

The right supplements can enhance the effects of the transition period. Here are some useful compounds.

Essential Fatty Acids   These include omega 3, which is found in fish oils, and GLA, which is found in evening primrose oil. A cheaper but less beneficial alternative is flaxseed oil. Essential fatty acids teach your body how to use fat as energy. In fact, research has shown that by adding them to a normal diet, you can enhance fat oxidation and lose adipose tissue while increasing lean mass.[9] One to 3 grams each of omega 3 and GLA a day is a good dose.

UTP, or Uridine   UTP supplements do to type 1 fibers what creatine does to type 2 fibers. This substance is one of the raw materials of DNA and is almost a sugar. Don't take more than 3 grams a day.

Ephedrine Plus Caffeine   Used before a workout, this supplement will force your body to use fat as energy.

Carnitine   Take 2 to 5 grams a day.

You may want to try one of the thermogenic fat burners, such as Muscle-Linc's Thermo Stak, which combine a number of ingredients for a synergistic fat-burning effect.

TRAINING DURING YOUR DIET

When you diet, your goal is to maintain the fat oxidation pathways as efficiently as possible. It's too late to develop them. Ideally, the transition period was a success and you're burning fat more easily. So you return to training with heavier weights and perform fewer high-repetition sets. You also reduce your training frequency.

The first training alteration is probably the most important. Once you arrive at the gym, warm up fully. The next step is to induce an intense, long-lasting muscle burn. That will lower your blood pH, which will within a few minutes stimulate the release of growth hormone, norepinephrine, and, possibly, testosterone.[10] Those hormones work synergistically to mobilize fat from the adipose tissue stores. They also force your body to oxidize fat as energy and so spare both muscle proteins and glycogen. That's the reason you want to stimulate their release as soon as possible in your workout. It's best to train early in the morning so that both your basal metabolic rate and fat oxidation are accelerated by the hormone compounds for the whole day. Using ephedrine plus caffeine or a thermogenic supplement one hour before your workout will stimulate both norepinephrine and testosterone release.

The following is a training schedule for the diet period:

Day 1: Chest and biceps, plus 1 100-rep set each for calves and triceps
Day 2: Quadriceps and abs, plus 1 100-rep set for hamstrings

Day 3: Shoulders and some aerobics, plus 1 100-rep set for back

Day 4: Rest

Day 5: Back and triceps, plus 1 100-rep set each for shoulders and biceps

Day 6: Hamstrings and calves, plus 1 100-rep set each for quads and chest

Day 7: Rest

Day 8: Repeat Day 1

This is for your normal heavy training. Don't forget to finish training each muscle group with 3 high-rep sets of an isolation exercise, 1 set of 30 reps, 1 of 50, and 1 of 75.

Continue taking the supplements you were using during the transition phase, along with vitamins, minerals, meal replacements, and so on.

High reps may seem strange at first, but once you get used to them, you'll want to end each workout with them. Otherwise, you'll feel that something's missing. If it seems painful at first, that only means your muscles aren't good at it, a sign that they're untrained with respect to type 1 fibers. It only points out how much they really need those high-rep sets.

References

1. B. Saltin, "Myosin Heavy Chain Isoforms in Single Fibers from M. Vastus Lateralis of Sprinters: Influence of Training," *Acta Physiol Scand* 151: 135 (1994).

2. A. L. Macnair, "Postprandial Lipid Partitioning and Obesity," *Proc Nutr Soc* 56: 194A (1997).

3. P. D. Berk, "How Do Long-Chain Free Fatty Acids Cross Cell Membranes?" *Proc Soc Exp Biol* 212: 1 (1996).

4. F. Kamp, "Fatty Acid Flip-Flop in Phospholipid Bilayers is Extremely Fast," *Biochemistry* 34: 11928 (1995).

5. K. D. Garlid, "Inactive Fatty Acids are Unable to Flip-Flop Across the Lipid Bilayer," *FEBS Lett* 408: 161 (1997).

6. B. Kiens, "Skeletal Muscle Substrate Utilization During Submaximal Exercise in Man: Effect of Endurance Training," *J Physiol (Lond)* 469: 459 (1993).

7. D. A. Pan, "Skeletal Muscle Triglyceride Levels Are Inversely Related to Insulin Action," *Diabetes* 46: 983 (1997).

8. B. Kiens, "Effect of Endurance Training on Fatty Acid Metabolism: Local Adaptations," *Med Sci Sports Exerc* 29: 640 (1997).

9. C. Couet, "Effect of Dietary Fish Oil on Body Fat Mass and Basal Fat Oxidation in Healthy Adults," *Int J Obesity* 21: 637 (1997).

10. S. F. Davies, "Influence of Acid-Base Status on Plasma Catecholamines During Exercise in Normal Humans," *American Journal of Physiology* 258: R1411 (1990).

FAT-BURNING TRANSITION WORKOUT (15 TO 30 DAYS BEFORE YOUR DIET BEGINS)

Day 1
Chest (heavy) and back (high rep)

Decline presses (warm-up)	2 × 10–12

Superset

Decline presses	2 × 6–8
Rowing machine	2 × 30, 50
Weighted dips (warm-up)	2 × 15

Superset

Weighted dips	2 × 10
Kneeling pulldowns	2 × 75, 100
Cable crossovers	3 × 30, 50, 75

Front delts (high rep), rear delts (high rep), and lateral delts (high rep)

Superset

Cable front raises	2 × 30, 50
Rear-delt machine	2 × 75, 100

Superset

Cable upright rows	2 × 75, 100
Machine lateral raises	2 × 30, 50

Biceps (heavy) and triceps (high rep)
Superset

Curls	2–4 × 6–12
Pushdowns	2–4 × 30, 50, 75, 100

Day 2
Quadriceps (heavy) and hamstrings (high rep)

Leg presses (warm-up)	3 × 10–12

Superset

Leg presses	2 × 6–8
Lying leg curls	2 × 30, 50
Squats (warm-up)	2 × 10–12

Superset

Squats	2 × 6–8
Seated leg curls	2 × 75, 100
Leg extensions	3 × 30, 50, 75

Calves (high rep) and abs (high rep)
Superset

Donkey calf raises	2 × 30, 50
Crunches	2 × 30, 50

Superset

Donkey calf raises	2 × 75, 100
Ab machine	2 × 75, 100

Day 3: Rest

Day 4
Back (heavy) and chest (high rep)

Bent-over barbell rows (warm-up)	2 × 10–12

Superset

Bent-over barbell rows	2 × 6–8
Dumbbell flyes	2 × 30, 50
Weighted chins (warm-up)	2 × 10–12

Superset

Weighted chins	2 × 6–8
Cable crossovers	2 × 75, 100
Kneeling pulldowns	3 × 30, 50, 75

Front delts (high rep), rear delts (high rep), and lateral delts (high rep)

Superset

Cable front raises	2 × 30, 50
Rear-delt machine	2 × 75, 100

Superset

Cable upright rows	2 × 75, 100
Machine lateral raises	2 × 30, 50

Biceps (high rep) and triceps (heavy)
Superset

Cable curls	2–4 × 30, 50, 75, 100
One-arm triceps extensions	2–4 × 6–12

Day 5
Hamstrings (heavy) and quadriceps (high rep)

Seated leg curls (warm-up)	2 × 10–12

Superset

Seated leg curls	3 × 6–8
Hack squats	2 × 30, 50
Stiff-legged deadlifts (warm-up)	3 × 10–15

Superset

Stiff-legged deadlifts	2 × 6–8
Leg extensions	2 × 75, 100

Calves (high rep) and abs (high rep)
Superset

Donkey calf raises	2 × 30, 50
Crunches	2 × 30, 50

Superset

Donkey calf raises	2 × 75, 100
Ab machine	2 × 75, 100

Day 6: Rest

Day 7
Chest (high rep) and back (high rep)
Superset

Dumbbell flyes	2 × 30, 50
Rowing machine	2 × 30, 50

Superset

Cable crossovers	2 × 75, 100
Kneeling pulldowns	2 × 30, 50

Front delts (heavy), rear delts (high rep), and lateral delts (high rep)

Partial barbell presses* (warm-up)	2 × 10–12

Superset

Partial barbell presses*	2 × 6–8
Rear-delt machine	2 × 75, 100
Machine front presses (warm-up)	2 × 10–12

Superset

Machine front presses	2 × 6–8
Machine lateral raises	2 × 30, 50

Greg Blount.

Biceps (high rep) and triceps (high rep)
Superset

| Cable curls | 4 × 30, 50, 75, 100 |
| Pushdowns | 4 × 30, 50, 75, 100 |

*Don't go below your neck.

Day 8
Quadriceps (high rep) and hamstrings (high rep)
Superset

| Hack squats | 2 × 30, 50 |
| Lying leg curls | 2 × 30, 50 |

Superset

| Leg extensions | 2 × 75, 100 |
| Seated leg curls | 2 × 75, 100 |

Calves (heavy) and abs (high rep)

| Standing calf raises (warm-up) | 2 × 10–15 |

Superset

Standing calf raises	2 × 4–8
Crunches	2 × 30–50
Seated calf raises (warm-up)	2 × 10–12

Superset

| Seated calf raises | 2 × 6–8 |
| Ab machine | 2 × 75–100 |

Day 9: Rest

Day 10
Chest (high rep) and back (high rep)
Superset

| Dumbbell flyes | 2 × 30, 50 |
| Rowing machine | 2 × 30, 50 |

Superset

| Cable crossovers | 2 × 75, 100 |
| Kneeling pulldowns | 75, 100 |

Front delts (high rep), rear delts (heavy), and lateral delts (heavy)

Bent-over laterals (warm-up)	2 × 12–15

Superset

Cable front raises	2 × 30, 50
Bent-over laterals	2 × 8–10
Lateral raises (warm-up)	2 × 10–12

Superset

Cable upright rows	2 × 75, 100
Lateral raises	2 × 8–10

Biceps (high rep) and triceps (high rep)

Superset

Cable curls	4 × 30, 50, 75, 100
Pushdowns	4 × 30, 50, 75, 100

Day 11

Quadriceps (heavy) and hamstrings (high rep)

Leg presses (warm-up)	3 × 10–12

Superset

Leg presses	2 × 6–8
Lying leg curls	2 × 30, 50
Squats (warm-up)	2 × 10–12

Superset

Squats	2 × 6–8
Seated leg curls	2 × 75, 100
Leg extensions	3 × 30, 50, 75

Calves (high rep) and abs (high rep)

Superset

Donkey calf raises	2 × 30, 50
Crunches	2 × 30, 50

Superset

Donkey calf raises	2 × 75, 100
Ab machine	2 × 75, 100

Day 12: Rest

When you feel tired, take an extra day of rest.

Try to rest less than one minute between sets. During the first days, if you feel the pace is too fast, you can rest longer. After a while you should get used to the faster pace.

BALANCED FAT-TO-MUSCLE DIET

Meal 1

8 ounces (2 percent) milk
Protein powder (stirred into milk)
3 rice cakes with peanut butter (2 tablespoons)
Totals: 560 calories; 40 grams of protein; 27 grams of fat; 40 grams of carbs
Macronutrient Percentages: Protein 30 percent; fat 40 percent; carbs 30 percent

Meal 2

Fat-to-Muscle Shake* (or meal replacement)
Totals: 456 calories; 44 grams of protein; 8 grams of fat; 52 grams of carbs
Macronutrient Percentages: Protein 40 percent; fat 15 percent; carbs 45 percent

Meal 3

6 ounces roasted skinless chicken
6 ounces lima beans
1 cup rice
Totals: 524 calories; 54 grams of protein; 8 grams of fat; 59 grams of carbs
Macronutrient Percentages: Protein 41 percent; fat 14 percent; carbs 45 percent

Meal 4

8 ounces cottage cheese (regular)
4 halves canned pears in juice
Totals: 340 calories; 30 grams of protein; 8 grams of fat; 36 grams of carbs
Macronutrient Percentages: Protein 37 percent; fat 21 percent; carbs 42 percent

Meal 5

Fat-to-Muscle Shake* (or meal replacement)
Totals: 456 calories; 44 grams of protein; 8 grams of fat; 52 grams of carbs
Macronutrient Percentages: Protein 40 percent; fat 15 percent; carbs 45 percent

Meal 6

Tuna sandwich on whole-wheat bread
($^1/_4$ cup tuna packed in water)

1 medium apple

1 ounce peanuts

Totals: 497 calories; 33 grams of protein;
11 grams of fat; 64 grams of carbs

Macronutrient Percentages: Protein
27 percent; fat 20 percent; carbs
53 percent

Grand Totals: 2,833 calories; 245 grams
of protein; 70 grams of fat; 303 grams
of carbs

Macronutrient Percentages: Protein
35 percent; fat 22 percent; carbs
43 percent

*The Fat-to-Muscle Shake includes: 9 ounces lowfat yogurt (any flavor), 1 cup milk (2 percent fat), egg or whey protein powder (enough to total 20 grams of protein), ice cubes for texture (optional), water to thin (if necessary). Blend until all ingredients are thoroughly combined and mixture is thick but still liquid.

Important: For best results, decrease calories by 50 to 100 per week by reducing portions—for example, half a Fat-to-Muscle Shake instead of the full serving—so the macronutrient percentages remain fairly constant. Once you're down to 2,000 calories, gradually begin to increase your aerobics to burn off more fat.

Chapter 26

DRUG-FREE OR DIE

BY PETER SISCO

Most of you have heard of the tragic death of Andreas Munzer. Munzer was 31 years old and died of a stomach hemorrhage. Not long before Munzer, Mohammed "Momo" Benaziza, another IFBB pro, died suddenly, and diuretics were reported to be the cause. These two cases are just the tip of the iceberg, however.

Remember the days when someone would see a big guy in the gym and say, "He must be on steroids." Well, steroids don't even begin to tell the story today. Take all the steroids your body can tolerate, and you won't even qualify for a pro contest, let alone win.

In his excellent article in the February '96 issue of *Muscular Development* John Romano provides a sweeping but not exhaustive list of drugs used by bodybuilders, including more than 35 different drugs in 18 categories. What categories? Diuretics, amphetamines, blood platelet aggregation inhibitors, thyroid hormones, blood viscosity conditioners, estrogen antagonists, and on and on. Don't forget that all of these are taken in addition to the bedrock of testosterone, human growth hormone, insulin, and a grab bag of garden-variety steroids. If these guys *still* have a lagging bodypart, they just inject some Esiclene directly into the muscle, and it swells up as if it had been hit with a baseball bat. Then it stays that way right through judging.

When my friend and coauthor John Little was writing for Weider, he met virtually all the top pro bodybuilders and most of the amateurs. Like everybody else who covers the sport, John knew full well that drugs are an everyday fact of life in bodybuilding. Once he asked a pro what the man took in the off-season. Here's the list, transcribed exactly from the pro's handwritten note:

Off-season
600 mg cyp. every other day
300 mg test. susp. every other day
10 Dianabol every day
4 Andadrol every day
10–20 clenbuterol every day
1 oz. marijuana per week
This is nonstop—no time off.

Six weeks out
1 Parabolin + 1 Primo Depo T every
  other day
3 cc test. susp. every other day
50 mg Halotestin
2 Fastin a day
20–25 clenbuterol a day
Percadan as needed
1 oz. marijuana per week

It's quite a picture, huh? And, while the man who takes these very drugs made it into the IFBB, he's never won a pro contest. Translation: *He isn't taking enough drugs to win.*

If you're thinking of trying this yourself, don't. Take that many drugs and you won't wake up tomorrow morning. It takes years to build up a tolerance to this kind of dosage; some never do, so they can't compete in the top ranks of the sport—like the pro who took the above list of drugs. Twenty-five clenbuterol a day? The next time you take a vitamin, pour 25 of them into your hand and imagine that's your daily overdose of only 1 of the 10 illegal drugs you're taking. Many of the others have to be injected.

Have you ever read a wordy defense of steroid use in a bodybuilding book or magazine that quoted medical studies showing no harmful side effects? That occurs because, when responsible physicians perform clinical studies, they don't give subjects 20 times the recommended dosage and they don't keep them on the drugs for five years. Moreover, no doctor this side of the Nazi Joseph Mengele would put a patient on an overdose of 15 to 20 drugs for years on end. There will never be any clinical studies to document the side effects of this pro's diabolic stack—but take your choice: cancer, leukemia, kidney failure, liver damage, testicular atrophy, sterility, or chromosome damage are virtually inevitable.

DOES ANYBODY CARE?

Remember, folks, this is a professional sport, just like NBA basketball, PGA golf, and NHL hockey. Yet, the writers, photographers, editors, and owners of the muscle magazines and the judges, the promoters, and the other athletes all know that the competitors are juiced to the gills with more illegal drugs than a touring heavy metal band. They all know, and it's something they talk about.

They refer to the athletes as "juice monkeys" and other colorful pejoratives. They tell stories like the one about the pro who went into a double-biceps pose during prejudging and his muscles went into a spasm and locked up. Two colleagues had to pick him up and carry him off the stage like a stone sculpture, suspended in a horizontal position with his arms still helplessly locked in a double-biceps shot. Yuk, yuk, yuk.

The picture the bodybuilding editors, officials et al. present to the public is an entirely different story, however. Consider the scribe who writes a completely fictitious interview in which a champ attributes his win to XYZ Vanadyl and some worthless periodization training scheme using low intensity and six different exercises per muscle group.

As for the official rules of this professional sport, the IFBB states that drugs are illegal and that athletes will be tested. They never are, though, because everyone knows what would happen. How does that make the sport look? About as legitimate as pro wrestling—a carnival sideshow.

Imagine if the New York Yankees put 14 men on the field at every game—just blatantly cheated—and the umpires, managers, opposing players, broadcast announcers, sports writers, and fans all said nothing. Nobody yelled, "They're cheating. They've got more men on the field than the rules allow!" The game of baseball would be burlesqued and corrupted, the fans would lose interest, and the sport would lose all its credibility in the eyes of serious pro athletes. Does that sound familiar?

THE RESULTS

Bodybuilding is killing its own market. What happens when new people get interested in bodybuilding, perhaps as a way to increase their strength for another sport? They pick up one of the magazines and see that the guy on the cover, the guys in the ads, the guys in the gossip columns, and the guys in every contest are all huge, ripped, freaky mass monsters. And that, my friends, becomes the standard in their eyes—a standard built on $25,000 to $50,000 per year in black market drug use that is very likely to end in medical disaster, in either the short or long term. That's the standard to which they aspire.

If they're lucky, they don't find out that the reason they can't achieve their aspirations is that they're not on the juice—lucky because they just drop out of the sport and look for something else to achieve. That's a far better fate than going for the gold in pro bodybuilding.

So Momo dies, Munzer dies, and countless others are narrowly saved from death by the quick action of fellow competitors, hospital emergency physicians, and simple, blind luck. What does the world of pro bodybuilding do? It just opens up another can of bodybuilders.

And then there's the cruelest irony of all: The bodybuilders hate being on drugs—all of them. They know they're being exploited and pressured so that the big players in the sport can make more money off them due to their ever freakier physiques. "Win the next contest, and you'll get one-year contract to hold up cans of xyz Supplements in our ads," they're promised. Imagine being a serious athlete in a sport you love, having natural ability and superior genetics, as well as a mom and dad and friends who encourage you. Imagine busting your butt in the gym to squeeze every shred of potential from your body—and watching your diet like a supermodel—only to lose to a guy who won because he has a drug connection to a new growth hormone straight from the pharmaceutical company in Switzerland.

Plus, there's no court of appeal. At least when American athlete Carl Lewis lost a race and his world record was broken by Canadian Ben Johnson, Lewis could have Johnson drug-tested. As a result Johnson's illegally earned world record was erased, he was suspended from the sport, and Lewis prevailed. In bodybuilding, again, it's a different story. The pro bodybuilder who loses a contest can't ask Ben Weider or the IFBB to investigate. He can't blow the whistle in the bodybuilding magazines—the people who publish them already know.

The prevailing attitude is, screw the official rules—quit complaining and get a better drug dealer. If the IFBB started enforcing its own rules today, the physiques would be so affected that John Goodman could very well win the next pro contest.

The guy who does win gets a contract to lie about how the supplement du jour, which he's never taken, made him a champion. The loser just drops out of the sport. A few years and thousands of drug injections later the champ quits too. Then 10 years down the road neither of them has anything to remind him of the old days except the champ's regular trips to the oncologist to get his kidney tumors checked.

That's what drug use has done to bodybuilding.

Avoid every temptation to use drugs or hormones. Follow the natural training and diet guidelines in this book and enjoy a lifetime of health benefits and the admiration of others. Build a natural physique of which you can be proud!

INDEX